Bathtub Physics

Bathtub Physics

by Hy Ruchlis

General Editor: DONALD BARR

Illustrated by RAY SKIBINSKI -

17332

 HARCOURT, BRACE & WORLD, INC., NEW YORK

J
530
R

Curriculum-Related Books, selected and edited by
the School Department of Harcourt, Brace & World,
are titles of general interest for individual reading.

3/68

Contents

Introduction 1

What are eyes for? To see, of course.

And ears? To hear.

And fingers? To touch and feel and hold things.

You smell with your nose and taste with your tongue.

These are the main senses; they tell you what is going on in the world.

But, most important, you have a brain that remembers what your senses tell you. You can think about these sensations. You can learn what they mean. You can choose what kind of sensations to pay attention to and which not to notice.

Stop for a moment and listen. Suddenly you hear things you didn't notice before. Perhaps a bird is chirping in the distance, or water is dripping from a faucet, or the refrigerator motor is purring, or leaves are rustling in the wind. Were these sounds there before you noticed them? Of course. But the part of your brain that notices things was shut off, so you paid no attention to these sounds.

There is a special way of seeing, hearing, and feeling. It is called observing. When you observe, your brain tells your eyes what to look for and your ears what kinds of sounds to hear. Now the seeing becomes watching and the hearing becomes listening.

A hunter in the woods must learn how to observe so that he can find his prey. A detective must learn to observe clues to solve a crime. A scientist must learn how to observe things that happen so that he can discover new information.

If you want to be like a scientist then you will have to learn how to observe, just as you once learned how to walk and talk.

What will you use for a laboratory? Your bathtub is a good place to start. No fancy instruments are required. You won't be doing big investigations and experiments, just little ones. And you probably won't be discovering anything really new, although it may be new to *you*.

THE SCIENCE OF PHYSICS

This book is entitled *Bathtub Physics*. You know what a bathtub is. But what is physics?

Physics is a science. Think of it as the kind of science that deals with things in motion and with the forces, or pushes and pulls, that cause motion or change it.

You may wonder why such a strange combination was selected—bathtubs and physics. For one thing, bathtubs are familiar, or should be. And, as you know, many things happen in bathtubs. Water flows. People get in and water rises. Objects float or sink. Soap bubbles form. Light is reflected from the surface of the water and of the tub. People fall and get hurt. All of these actions—and more —involve energy, forces, and motions. They are part of the subject of physics.

A science always involves seeking to find out *why* things happen. In this book you will find out why many things happen in the bathtub. You may have noticed these happenings yourself. Perhaps as a result of reading this book you will begin to observe things that you never noticed before and wonder about actions and events that you never paid attention to before.

HOW INVESTIGATIONS BEGIN

There are many objects in your surroundings to which you pay no attention at all until something different happens to them. For example, if an ashtray resting on the table suddenly goes up in the air by itself, that would be good reason to launch an investigation. How did it happen? What caused it to happen? Can we make it go up and down at will?

Yet events don't have to be quite that dramatic to lead to an investigation. Perhaps one day an ashtray jiggles on the table. You hear a truck roll by in the street. This could be the start of a very interesting investigation involving the vibrations caused by the truck and the conditions under which ashtrays respond to such vibrations.

It is the same way with the bathtub. You fill it with water. You step in. You sit down. The water rises. It splashes around. Water waves move along the surface. The water gets dirty. When the drain is opened the tub empties. A whirlpool may form. All of these events, which you can easily observe, lead to questions, and each question can become an investigation.

READING AND DOING

And now for a brief note about the way to read this book. One way is to relax in an easy chair and read without interruption, following the investigations with your imagination. It is a good way. But perhaps you will wish to try another way. This book will describe certain actions that occur in the tub. There will often be questions that are intended to make you think. Suppose, when you read such questions, you stop for a while and try to think about the question. It will then be more fun to see how your thoughts match those in the book or differ with them. When the book mentions things that happen in the bathtub, it isn't quite practical to stop reading, remove your clothes, and take a bath to see if the book is correct. But the next time you take a bath you might see for yourself if the statements are correct. Or, in many cases you can make use of "little bathtubs"— sink, pots, pans, tumblers, and dishes.

Seeing for yourself is important for several reasons. First, it is the way scientists work. When one scientist reports some observations, others try to repeat what he did and check the observations themselves. If it seems to work for only one man, something is wrong. Only after a number of scientists have reported the same thing is it accepted as a fact.

Second, while you are testing an idea by trying it for yourself you may observe things happening that the book did not mention. These unexpected observations can lead to new discoveries and new knowledge. Keep your eyes and ears open when you repeat some investigation in the book. Then you are quite likely to make your own new discoveries.

The bathtub is usually not a dangerous place, but it can be if you are careless. Many people slip and fall in the bathtub—for reasons that we shall discuss later. Never move rapidly while standing in or near the tub, especially if the floor or tub is wet and slippery.

And do not use glass containers for any of your investigations. Dropping and breaking a glass object produces dangerous, jagged pieces that are hard to see against white tile floors. Use plastic or metal containers instead.

And now let's proceed.

Waves 2

Look down at a tub full of water when the surface is quiet. Then drop into the water a small heavy object such as a marble or a stone about an inch long. Immediately a wave forms around the point where the object hit the water and moves outward in a perfect circle.

If the object is large enough you may see a second and a third wave follow the first one—perhaps even a whole train of waves. The bathtub is a bit small for such an extensive train of waves to be formed, but you can observe one in a pond into which a large stone is thrown.

What causes a wave to form? When the object hits the water it begins to push the water down. But the water can't actually go down because some water already occupies the space below. There is only one place for the water to go to make way for the object—up and out, above the normal water level.

As a result, a small mound of water is raised all around the object. Some of the water may be pushed up so rapidly that it may break away from the surface and become an outward and upward splash.

How a wave is formed

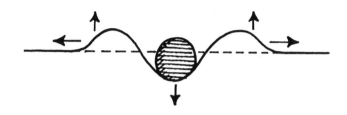

The heavy object sinks rapidly into the water, leaving an empty space above it. The mound of water, of course, does not stand still. Part of it falls back into the empty space left behind by the object.

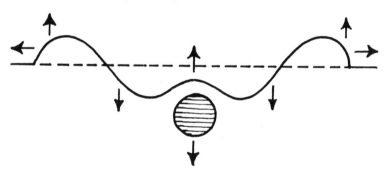

All the water around the spot where the object first hit the surface has been set into a complicated vibrating motion. Each bit of water moves up and down and causes the water in the neighboring region on both sides to move up and down, too, but not quite at the same moment. You can observe this up-and-down vibration by floating a cork or similar small object in still water. Then create a wave by dropping an object into the water. The cork bobs up and down as a wave goes by.

It takes a bit of time for the water at one place to make the nearby water move. Some parts of the water are made to move up while nearby parts of the water are moving down. You can observe this effect by floating a series of corks near each other in the bathtub. When you create a nearby wave, you find some corks moving up while others are moving down.

Why does the wave continue to move after the object causing it has come to rest? For example, a stone dropped into water falls to the bottom and comes to a stop. But the wave continues to move outward.

The water has been disturbed by the stone and has been set into vibrating motion. That vibrating motion then exists independently of whatever caused it. Vibrations travel outward with a speed that depends mainly on the nature of the material in which they are formed.

For liquids like honey or maple syrup, which are much more viscous than water and which flow more slowly, the speed of the wave would be greatly reduced. It would also die away much sooner.

Waves can be formed in other ways than by dropping sinking objects into a liquid like water. Floating objects also cause waves when dropped on the surfaces of liquids, but are less effective in causing waves. A wave can also be formed by moving a broad surface back and forth in the liquid.

Why not try these ways of making waves in the bathtub?

The palm of the hand makes a train of waves when

moved back and forth in the water. Proper timing is important, and with a bit of practice you can make an excellent train of waves. Form such a train of waves near the center of the tub. Watch what happens as the first wave reaches the side of the tub. It bounces back and travels in a different direction. In other words, it is reflected.

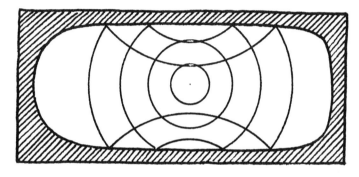

Reflection of water waves

Notice a surprising thing. The waves bouncing off the wall of the tub move through the new waves you continue to make with your hand. Each wave continues in its own direction, as if the oppositely moving wave were not there. This is an important fact about all waves. They can pass through each other without destroying each other.

Now try making waves by moving a plastic cup up and down on the water in a regular manner—in a definite rhythm. Notice the spacing between waves—this is called the wavelength. Then move the cup up and down with a faster rhythm. This time the waves come out spaced more closely—the wavelength is shorter. Make the rhythm slower. Now the waves come out spaced farther apart—the wavelength is longer.

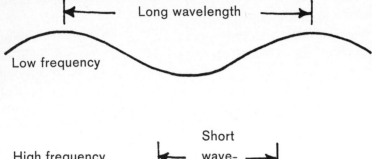

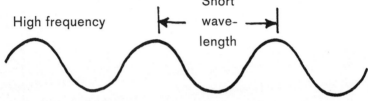

Relationship of frequency and wavelength

Suppose that you push the cup up and down once per second. The frequency, or rate of vibration, is 1 cycle per second, or 1 cps. If you push the cup up and down 2 times a second, then the frequency is 2 cps.

If you push the cup up and down 5 times a second, then the frequency of vibration is 5 cps. Since the frequency is greater than before, the distance between waves, or the wavelength, is less. In other words, a wave of higher frequency has a shorter wavelength.

The water waves you generate in the tub have rather *short* wavelengths and high frequency. Waves generated by a boat have much lower frequency (are not produced as often), and so the wavelengths are much longer.

Occasionally an earthquake will cause the surface of

the earth near or under the water to rise or fall suddenly. This causes a wave in the water, just as pushing the cup up and down causes a wave in the tub. But this wave has much greater dimensions. The wavelength may be many miles and the frequency may be only several an hour. This type of water wave with a very long wavelength can travel across the ocean. If the up-and-down motion, or amplitude, of the wave is large, the water may slowly rise many feet above its normal level and move over the land. Such a wave, known as a tsunami—sometimes incorrectly called a tidal wave—can cause great damage to towns and cities along the seacoast, thousands of miles from the source of the earthquake.

Now to return to the bathroom for a moment. Look around. See if you can detect any other waves besides those on the surface of water in the tub. They are there— several different kinds.

During the day there are light waves from the sun streaming through the window. At night, light waves stream out of the lamp bulb. Such light waves do not require a material like air or water. They can even travel through the space between the sun and the earth.

Scientists refer to these waves as electromagnetic because they are closely related to electricity and magnetism.

Wavelengths of visible light are very short—about 1/50,000 of an inch. Frequencies are very high—about 1 quadrillion (1,000,000,000,000,000) cps. Different colors of light waves have different wavelengths, ranging from about 1/30,000 of an inch for red light to about 1/65,000 of an inch for blue.

Bring a battery-operated radio into the bathroom and

turn it on. (**Never use a plug-in type of radio in the bathroom because of the danger of electric shocks in a wet room.**) You will hear a program that has been sent out on radio waves from a station many miles away. These waves had to pass through the walls of the room to reach the radio set.

Radio waves are also electromagnetic in nature, but of much longer wavelength and lower frequency than the light waves. Wavelengths of the radio waves that produce most radio programs are several hundred yards long and their frequencies are about 1 million cps.

Suddenly you may hear your mother's voice calling you. She is in the kitchen and you are quite far away, in the bathroom. How do you know what she wants? A sound wave, caused by vibration of the air, moved outward from her vocal cords and reached your ear. Such sound waves coming from the human voice are generally several feet long and have frequencies of several hundred cps.

Water waves of the kind you made in the tub may not seem very important in your everyday life, but waves in general are very important. Light waves are vital, not only to see with, but also because they are the basic source of energy for food-making by plants. Radio (and TV) waves are the basis of our modern system of long-distance communication. Sound waves are the basis of man's short-distance communication by means of speech. In the two chapters that follow you will investigate more fully several of these important types of waves. As before, the bathtub can serve as the starting point for such investigations.

Brain Teasers
Answers appear on page 113.

1. You observe a small boat anchored in the water of a bay, bobbing up and down once every 4 seconds as a water wave passes by. You also note that the distance between crests of successive waves is about the same as the length of a nearby 30-foot boat. What is the speed of the wave? How long will it take for the wave to reach the end of the bay about ¼ of a mile away?

2. What is the velocity of a radio wave if a station broadcasting at a frequency of 1 million cps generates waves with a wavelength of about 1,000 feet?

Investigations on Your Own

1. There may be a high point in your area that overlooks a lake or other large body of water. From that vantage point observe the waves generated by boats. Take photographs at intervals to study what happens.

2. Throw two stones into a quiet pond or lake. Observe the way the water waves move through each other.

3. Cover the side of a tub with a towel. Are water waves reflected from the towel in the same way they were from the tub? What happens with other materials, such as wood, metal, etc.?

Sounds 3

Close the drain and let water run into the bathtub rather slowly. Kneel on the floor—on a bathmat, of course—and put your ear firmly against the top of the tub at the end opposite from where the water is coming in. What do you hear? Lift your head and listen. Is the sound different? Repeat a few times to be sure.

Shut off the water and let it run out of the tub. Listen as you hold your ear to the top of the tub. Then lift your head and listen. Do you hear the noise of water running out of the tub? Do you hear it more clearly through the tub than through the air?

Apparently the sound of water comes through the solid material of the tub to your ear more clearly than through the air. How can that be?

Think of different situations in which sound is heard —a door bangs, a hammer hits a nail, a car moves, you walk across a hard floor, the string of a guitar is plucked. Motion of some kind is always the cause of sound.

If you tap a table, the top of the table is pushed and moves slightly. If you close the door, the wall is made to move slightly. When anything moves, it always causes objects it is touching to move, too.

Tables, walls, and most objects are solid and rigid. They don't visibly move when tapped or banged unless you give them an exceptionally strong wallop. But they are somewhat flexible. As a result, very slight back-and-forth motions, or vibrations, are set up whenever most objects are struck.

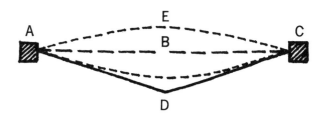

How a stretched string vibrates

A tightly stretched string or rubber band (ABC) illustrates the nature of a vibration. Suppose that you pull the middle of the string away from its normal resting position to position D. The string becomes stretched. When you let go, it is pulled back toward B. By the time the string gets back to its initial position at B it is moving rapidly. It tends to keep going on the other side, slowing down all the while until it comes to a stop at E. Again it is stretched and so is pulled back toward B. By the time the string gets back to its initial position at B it is moving quite rapidly. Once more it keeps going, and moves to an almost equal distance on the other side. Eventually, after many such vibrations the string comes to rest.

All solid, rigid objects vibrate in a somewhat similar manner when portions of them are suddenly pushed and made to move out of their normal positions.

When one part of an object vibrates it affects the rest of the object. The vibrating part pushes and pulls neighboring parts, which are also set into vibration with the same timing. Then the nearby parts set the parts near *them* in motion. This happens rapidly, in sequence. Thus, the effect of a sudden motion at one point in an object is transmitted from that source to all other parts in a widening circle, with the source as a center. The successive vibrations are all transmitted in the same way to every part of the solid object. This is how a sound wave travels through a solid material.

Now you can see why you heard the sound of the falling water hitting the tub when your ear was held close to the tub. The vibrations set up in the tub by the falling water made the solid material of the tub vibrate, and this vibration was transmitted through the material to your ear.

Why can you still hear the sound when you lift your ear? Nothing seems to be connecting the tub to your ear. But there is something—air. Air is a real material. It is made up of tiny particles called molecules, just as are water, steel, and all other materials. The molecules in air are spaced farther apart than in liquids or solids. As a result, air is lighter and more transparent than water or steel. But we would expect it to transmit sound waves because it has particles, molecules, that can move when pushed.

Air is a bouncy material, as shown by the fact that it is

used in automobile tires to reduce the bumpiness of the ride. This bounciness, or elasticity, makes air and other gases fairly good transmitters of vibrations in the form of waves. Consequently we can hear sound traveling through air as we do through solid materials.

Think back a moment to your investigation of sound in the tub. Falling water makes the solid material of the tub vibrate. Both the water and the tub cause the nearby air to vibrate. A sound wave moves through the air to your ear. Vibration of the air makes a flexible eardrum in your ear vibrate. Special nerves in the inner ear then send signals to the brain, informing it of the kind of sound reaching the eardrum. The brain analyzes the messages, and you become aware of the sound.

If sound vibrations pass through solids and through gases like air, can they also pass through liquids? If you get into a great big "bathtub"—a pool, for example— and put your head completely under water, you can easily hear a nearby swimmer splashing in the water. In a lake or ocean you can hear the noises of the motors of boats quite far away.

Sound travels through any material—solid, liquid, or gas. But sound won't travel through a vacuum, a region which completely lacks particles of any substance.

Could anyone on earth hear the sound of the engine of a space ship traveling in outer space? No, because there is practically nothing—no air or other material—to transmit the vibrations to the earth. Of course, we can pick up the sound inside the space ship, convert it to radio waves, transmit the radio waves to the earth, and convert them back to sound waves in a radio set. But in that case, sound is not being transmitted across space. Radio waves are being transmitted, and these waves are of a different kind from sound waves.

SINGING IN THE BATHROOM

Do you like to sing in the bathtub? Well, if you don't, many other people do, and for an interesting reason.

It isn't the bath*tub* that's important in this activity. It's the bath*room* (or shower stall) that counts. So you won't have to get into the tub for this investigation.

Try singing (the best you can) in the bathroom with the door closed. Then go into a larger room and try it there. Or, better still, try singing a song or two outdoors, with nobody within hearing distance, if you prefer.

In the bathroom your voice sounds rich and resounding. The volume of sound is much greater, and certain tones you sing seem especially loud and full.

If you happen to have an enclosed shower stall at home, be sure to test your singing voice inside that narrow space. Your voice now seems to be as rich and as loud as that of an opera singer. Why does singing in the small shower stall or bathroom seem so much better than it does outdoors, or even in a large room? A musician would describe the sound as more resonant, because it sounds louder, fuller, and richer. One reason for that has to do with the way sound waves in air bounce off hard solid objects like the walls, ceilings, and floors of the bathroom. Another reason is related to the nature of a musical sound in contrast with a noise.

Let us consider the nature of a sound wave in greater detail. Imagine a sound wave coming out of your mouth and traveling toward the wall, as shown by the dotted line moving toward A. When the sound wave hits the wall the moving air in the vibration is stopped and piles up slightly. Then, like a spring, it bounces back, or is reflected, and starts moving in the opposite direction, as shown by the dotted lines at B. It soon reaches the opposite wall and bounces off again, as shown at C and D.

In the meantime other vibrations have come out of the mouth and add to the volume of the sound. In a short while the new sound waves that are being formed, added to the old ones bouncing off the walls, build up the in-

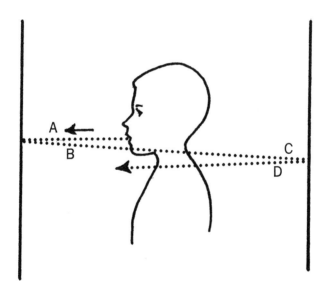

Reflection of sound waves from the walls

tensity of the vibrations and make the sound much louder than it would normally be. Outside, in a large open field, the sound simply spreads out in all directions without ever reflecting (bouncing) back to your ears.

Inside, hard walls of the bathroom or shower stall make a good reflecting surface. Some of the intensity of a vibration is lost with each reflection from a hard surface. But most of it is reflected. Soft rugs, or draperies on a window, would stop practically all reflection, just as they would stop a ball from bouncing. As a result, a room with a rug, soft furniture coverings, and draperies would not give the same loudness by reflection as does a bathroom with hard walls. Try singing in a room with a rug and soft furniture and see for yourself.

Now try this in the bathroom. Sing or hum a tone as low in pitch as you can produce. Then gradually raise the pitch, higher and higher and higher, as high as you can go. On the way up the scale you find several particular musical tones that become louder than the rest. These are said to be resonating. What causes this resonating effect? The answer involves understanding the difference between a musical sound and a noise.

In the previous chapter you observed that when a regular vibration is set up in water—perhaps by moving the palm back and forth—the wave has a definite frequency that depends upon the rate of the vibration. With such a regular vibration there is a definite distance between waves, in other words, a definite wavelength. Also, you observed in water waves that a greater frequency produces more frequent waves, which are closer together and thereby have shorter wavelengths. Thus, high frequency and short wavelength go together.

But suppose the motion of the palm is not regular, and you swish the water about at random. In that case, choppy waves are produced that have no definite wavelength or frequency.

The situation with regard to sound waves is somewhat similar. The wave for a musical sound has the same kind of regularity as a water wave produced by regular motions of the palm, while a noise has the same kind of irregularity of vibration as a choppy wave produced by swishing the palm in the water at random.

If you pluck the string of a guitar, you will see from the blurred appearance of the string that it vibrates back and forth rapidly. This vibration is very regular. One string may be vibrating 200 times a second. Another may vibrate 232 times a second. Still another might vibrate 1,050 times a second. Each number of vibrations produces a certain tone in the musical scale.

If the vibration rate of a certain guitar string is 200 times a second, this means that each vibration of the string follows the previous one $\frac{1}{200}$ of a second later. The vibrations of a string are so regular that they could be used to keep time in accurate clocks. In fact, one type of watch recently produced keeps time not by the regular vibrations of a spring or of a pendulum, but by the vibrations of a tiny tuning fork that produces a faint musical tone.

The rate of vibration of a pendulum in a grandfather's clock and of the spring in a watch are too slow to be heard by us as musical tones. Not until the vibrations reach about 20 per second (20 cycles per second) can most people hear the sound as a very low-pitched musical tone. The lowest tone on a piano—on the left end of the keyboard—vibrates at the rate of 27 cycles per second. Keys at the middle of the piano produce tones that vibrate several hundred times a second. The high tones produced by the keys near the right end of the keyboard vibrate several thousand cycles per second. At 10,000 cycles per second, some older people can no longer hear the musical tone. At 20,000 cycles per second, the musical sound becomes inaudible to all human beings, although dogs, bats, porpoises, and other animals can still hear such tones.

Animal trainers can perform unusual tricks with dogs using small whistles that produce sounds with more than 20,000 cps. For example, one can train a dog to "count" objects, not by observation and reasoning, but by teaching it to bark every time the special whistle is blown out of sight of the audience. An unseen person blows the whistle the number of times equal to the proper count, and the dog barks correspondingly. The audience can then be fooled into believing that the dog can count.

A sound is musical and has definite pitch only if the vibration has some regularity, as pictured in A and B (facing page). A noise (C) is just a jumble of vibrations that have no regularity. As a result, it has no definite pitch.

When you slap a wall with your palm, the sound is a mixture of vibrations from many sources. Air is squeezed out from between the palm and wall, and this sets up one kind of vibration. The hand vibrates and causes different vibrations. The wall is made of various materials—perhaps plaster, wood, or metal—and this complex structure has its own vibrations. The combination is then a jumble of vibrations, which we hear as a noise. But when you sing a note of definite pitch, the vocal

Wavelengths of different sounds

A — Pure musical tone

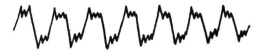

B — Musical tone with extra tones (overtones)

C — Noise

cords in your throat vibrate regularly, like the strings of a violin, and produce evenly timed sound waves. The same regular vibration rate is found in all musical instruments, whether the vibrations are caused by strings, as in a violin, or by air, as in a flute.

Suppose that you sing a tone so that your vocal cords vibrate 200 times a second. This means that a pulse of air moves out of your mouth every $\frac{1}{200}$ of a second.

Sound waves travel with a certain definite, regular speed in each material. For air, the speed of sound waves is about 1,100 feet per second. What happens when we make a musical sound of 200 cps? By the time the second vibration comes out, the first vibration has moved $\frac{1}{200}$ of 1,100 feet, or 5.5 feet. The third vibration comes out

⅟₂₀₀ of a second later, also 5.5 feet behind. All successive waves come out evenly spaced, 5.5 feet apart. The wavelength of this wave is said to be 5.5 feet, as shown in A.

On the other hand, suppose you sing a higher tone, producing 550 vibrations per second. Then the waves come out ⅟₅₅₀ × 1,100 feet, or 2 feet apart, a distance that is much less than the 5.5-foot spacing of the sound wave from the 200-vibration-per-second sound. The wavelength of the tone of higher pitch is therefore shorter, as shown in B.

Sound waves of different frequencies

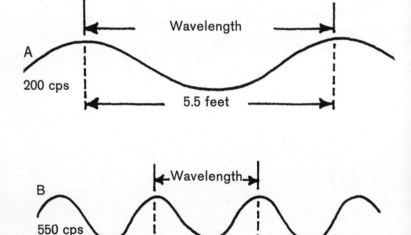

Now suppose that the tone of 200 cycles per second, of wavelength 5.5 feet, is being produced in a box or room that is 5.5 feet long, exactly the same as its wavelength. In that case each wave will bounce back and forth between the walls and pass by the mouth, the source of the sound, at exactly the same moment that a new vibration comes out. This causes the old wave to reinforce the new one. The effect then builds up, and loud resonating sounds are produced.

If the size of the box or room is somewhat more or less than 5.5 feet, then the timing is no longer perfect. Each vibration passes the mouth out of step with the new one coming out, and may actually interfere with it, thereby reducing the intensity of vibration.

For this reason the tone of 550 vibrations per second, with its 2-foot wavelength, would find a 5.5-foot box or room to be the wrong size to bring the reflected waves in step with the new sound waves coming out of the mouth. A 2-foot box would be just right for that sound wave. Each box resonates best to certain tones whose wavelengths correspond to the size of the box.

The particular sizes of resonating rooms or boxes mentioned in the previous section are not the only ones that resonate to the tones of 200 and 550 cycles per second. Actually, a box half or twice or four times the resonating sizes mentioned will give perfect timing and will also resonate. And remember, too, that in a box—or a bathroom—there are different distances across the length, width, and height of the room. Vibrations can also bounce off curved surfaces like the tub itself. Your bathroom may resonate to a whole series of tones.

When you sing in a larger room it takes a longer time for the sounds to reach the walls and bounce off, and the sounds are weakened as they spread out over longer distances. The room is also the wrong size for resonating to the normal tones we sing. For example, a big living room might resonate very well to the lowest tone that an organ can play because the wavelength of such a tone may be 20 to 30 feet. But the room is too big to resonate to the sound from your vocal cords when they produce vibrations with wavelengths about 1 to 3 feet long.

Well then, wouldn't a small box be a better resonator for you than a bathroom? Why not try it? Get a cardboard carton that is closed on all sides. Cut a round hole about 2 or 3 inches in diameter on one of the broad sides. Sing into the opening, starting at the lowest pitch and going gradually up the scale to the highest. Do you observe that the hollow box resonates to any particular tones?

Try this with a milk bottle, soda bottle, or jar. Do they resonate to different tones?

You may be surprised that something as small as a milk bottle can resonate to a musical tone. In this type of situation, in which the sound is being produced outside the resonating chamber, it happens that the smallest resonating size is one fourth of the wavelength. For a normal tone, say one of a 3-foot wavelength, a bottle ¾ of a foot, or 9 inches, tall would actually resonate best.

Did you ever wonder why the box of a violin or a cello has such a strange shape? This shape is designed so that each vibration of a musical sound can find its own resonating length in some particular direction in the box. Very high-pitched tones of short wavelength find their proper lengths up and down along the short thickness of the violin box. Tones of medium pitch find their proper resonating lengths along the medium-sized width of the violin. Low tones of long wavelength find their proper resonating lengths along the length of the box. The Sshaped holes on the upper side of the violin under the strings are the places where the resonating sounds from the box get out into the air and begin to travel outward toward the listeners.

Why is the resonating box for a cello much bigger than that for a violin? The strings of a cello are longer, heavier, and looser, and therefore vibrate more slowly than those of a violin. The cello thus produces low-pitched musical sounds that are of low frequency and have long wavelengths. But these long-wavelength sound waves require larger resonating chambers. In order to match the sound waves being produced, the resonating box of a cello must be correspondingly larger than that of a violin.

In an instrument like the marimba, the tones are produced when a series of separate vibrating bars of different size at the top of the instrument are struck with a hammer. Below each vibrating bar is a hollow resonating chamber that makes the sound from the bar much louder.

How did we ever get from the bathroom to violins? Ah! That's one of the mysteries of science. The principles of science have an interesting way of applying to everything around us, including bathrooms, milk bottles, and violins.

Brain Teasers
Answers appear on page 114.

1. Why should music produced by an orchestra in a large auditorium sound a bit different when the auditorium is filled with people than when it is empty?

2. A peal of thunder begins 25 seconds after you observe the distant flash. How far away was the lightning flash?

3. How far away is a cliff that produces an echo 1.3 seconds after you shout toward it?

Investigations on Your Own

1. It was stated on page 23 that the speed of a sound wave in air is about 1,100 feet per second. How could you prove that with actual measurement?

Why not try to measure the speed of sound?

2. A large building near an open field with a slight rise in it provides a good situation for studying echoes. Stand about 20 feet from the side of the building and shout at it. Do you hear an echo? Try it at 40 feet, 60 feet, 80 feet, 100 feet. Use a yardstick to measure the distance or estimate it by pacing the distance.

At what distance do you begin to hear an echo? Can you explain why there is a definite minimum distance for an echo?

3. Would you expect the speed of sound waves in air to be the same at high altitudes as those at sea level? Would it be the same in a steel rail as in water? As in air? Would it be faster or slower in air? You may want to read in the library about the speed of sound in various materials. You might find out how to apply what you learn to the sonar system of locating objects under water. A similar system is used by porpoises and bats to locate objects in the dark.

Light Beams   4

In the previous two chapters you investigated two forms
of waves—those produced in water, and sound waves.
Now let us turn our attention to another form of waves—
those of light.

Let some water run into the tub until it is a few inches
deep. Shut off the water and wait a few minutes until
all the waves die down. Look straight down. There's your
mirror image, as clear as can be, although a bit on the
dim side. Brighten the image by shining a flashlight toward your face.

Stir the water gently with your finger. Watch the distorted image dance about and then gradually become
still. Now the image is back to its original shape. Splash
the water harder. This time the image completely dis-
appears.

Why does the surface of water form a mirror image?
Why is it dimmer than the image in a regular mirror?
Why does a flashlight shining on your face make the

image brighter? Why does the image disappear when the water surface is made rough?

A good way to begin investigation of these questions is to shine a flashlight at the surface of the water in a darkened bathroom. A penlight is best because the light comes out from a sharp point and forms a distinct beam. But a regular flashlight will also do. In any case, attach a cardboard tube about a foot or more long to the front of the flashlight. If no tube is available make one out of sheets of paper by rolling them into a tube and fastening the edge with gummed tape.

A penlight shining through such a tube creates an almost straight beam of light, as shown. Now you can direct the beam down at the surface of the water and see what happens to it.

First, hold the flashlight at an angle. Does any of the light in the beam reflect from (bounce off) the water

Reflection of light from a water surface

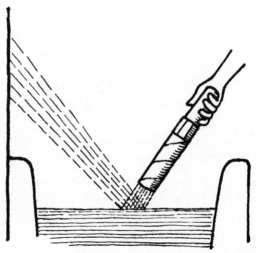

surface? There are several ways to tell. One way is to observe the spot of light on the wall near the tub. Sometimes you may be able to see the reflected beam, especially if there is any dust in the air. You might try making some clean dust by sprinkling fine talcum powder into the air above the reflected beam. Or, if someone in your family smokes, ask him to blow some smoke at the reflected beam. The particles of dust or smoke in the air reflect light to your eye and make the beam visible.

You might also try placing your hand near the spot where the beam of light hits the water. A bright spot on the lower part of your hand reveals the location of the reflected beam of light. You can then move your hand up so as to locate the beam, until it reaches the bright spot on the wall.

Observe the angle at which the beam strikes the water surface. Then observe the angle at which the beam is reflected. The talcum powder or smoke method of showing the beam is best for this purpose. Do you observe anything about the angle at which the beam strikes the surface of the water and the angle at which it is reflected? You will find that the angles are equal.

Try changing the angles. The drawings show some typical reflections. When the light beam strikes the water at a glancing angle, as in A, the reflection comes off the surface at a similar glancing angle. When the angle be-

Three typical reflections

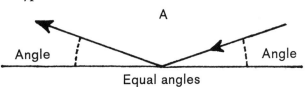

A

Angle   Angle

Equal angles

tween the light beam and the water surface is larger, as in B, then the reflected beam bounces off at a larger angle. And when the beam goes almost straight down, as in C, it bounces back almost straight up.

Three typical reflections (cont.)

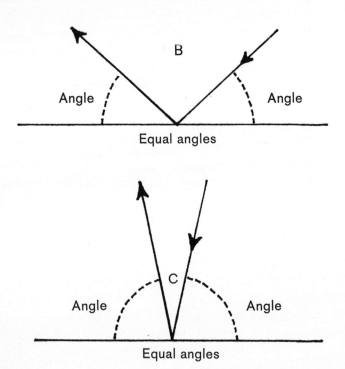

Now try this. Shine the flashlight downward at an angle to the water and produce a spot of light on the wall. At the same time roughen the surface of the water a bit by stirring it with a finger. What happens to the nice, clear reflected spot on the wall? Watch it broaden out, become distorted and blurred, and dance around.

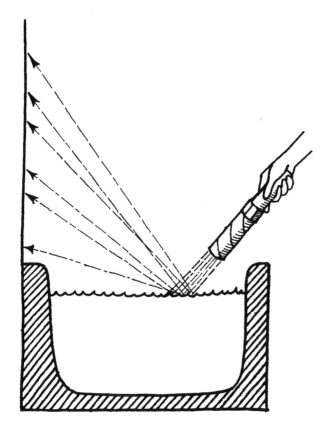

Reflection of light from rough water

The many rays (narrow beams) of light from the flashlight all strike the water at about the same angle. If the water is still, and therefore flat, then the light rays are all reflected at equal angles. So they bounce off together and the beam stays together. That's why a concentrated spot is formed on the wall if the water is smooth.

When you stir the water, the surface becomes wavy. The reflected rays still bounce off at the same angle with which the rays hit each bit of water, but now each part of the surface is constantly changing position. This causes any particular light ray to strike the water at a constantly changing angle and to bounce off to constantly changing places on the wall. The light beam dances around and broadens out depending on how much commotion there is on the surface.

So you see that only smooth surfaces can make concentrated reflections. Rough surfaces tend to broaden, or diffuse, the reflections in all directions.

What causes the surface to form mirror images? Suppose a person is looking down at the water to see a reflection of a small object (A). His eye (B) is shown greatly enlarged so that we can observe exactly what happens to the light. Assume that rays of light from the sun shine on the object and are reflected from it.

Most objects are not as smooth as the surfaces of quiet water or of mirrors. In fact, imperfections of only 1/10,000 of an inch in a surface are sufficiently large to bounce light off in all directions. Imagine that the object at A has such imperfections. As a result, some of the light rays from the sun—such as C and D—are reflected from the object. They bounce off the water surface as shown at E and F and eventually enter the eye (B).

Notice how rays C and D spread apart as they move downward at an angle toward the water. When they are reflected from the surface, each at its own angle, they continue to spread apart until they enter the eye.

The eye has no way of knowing where the rays are really coming from. They seem to be coming from point

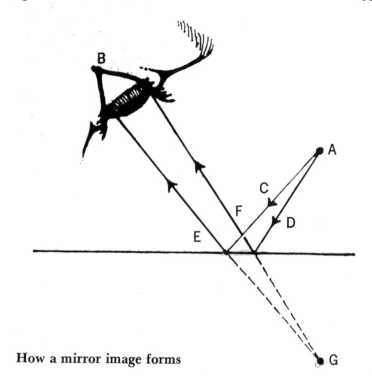

How a mirror image forms

G, below the surface of the water. In other words the eye sees a copy, or image, of the object beneath the surface of the water.

Most objects are larger than the one shown at A. However, the reasoning is still the same. Each point on the large object produces its own image. All of the images of the points in the objects are combined by the eye into a single large image that looks like the original large object.

Of course, to produce this image there must be a very smooth reflecting surface that enables the rays to bounce off in such a manner that they keep the same relationship to one another, after reflecting, as before. A smooth, flat surface does this very nicely. A roughened surface spoils the mirror image because it sends the light rays bouncing off helter-skelter in all directions.

Any smooth surface will reflect light the way smooth water does. Most mirrors are made of highly reflective silver (or other metal) coated on very smooth glass. A highly polished table or floor shows mirror reflections. So does a glass window. The shiny body of a car also produces mirror images. However, the curved surface of the car reflects light at different angles than a flat surface does. As a result, the image looks distorted.

Why is the image in the water dimmer than it is in a regular mirror? There are several reasons for that. Shine the flashlight into the water of a full tub. Is all the light reflected? No, some of it—in fact, most of it—enters the water and illuminates the bottom of the tub.

The portion of light energy reflected from the water is very small—only about 10 percent. The reverse is true in a mirror. The metal at the back of the mirror reflects most of the light that hits it—about 95 percent. Therefore the images seen in a regular mirror are much brighter than those from water surfaces.

A second reason for the darker image in water is that your head blocks illumination from reaching your face. Light from an overhead lamp or from sunlight shining into the window can reach your face only indirectly by reflection from the walls, from the floor, or from the tub. Since there isn't much illumination on your face, the reflection is dim.

When you shine a flashlight at your face, some of the

light is reflected and goes downward to the water to make a brighter image.

A BENT STRAIGHT STICK

What happens to the light that is not reflected from the surface of the water in the bathtub? Try this. Fill the tub to its normally full position. Then put a straight stick into the water at an angle. If you look at the stick, you will see that it no longer appears straight. The part in the water seems to bend upward.

Pull the stick out of the water slightly. Again the exposed part is completely straight and the part in the water is bent upward.

A stick looks bent in water.

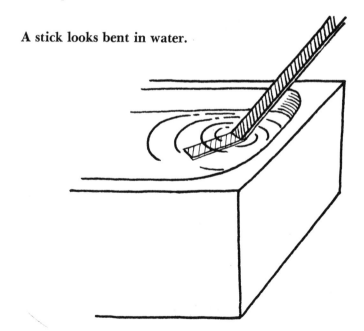

Take the stick completely out of the water. It appears to be its normal straight self again. The bend has completely straightened out.

Obviously, the stick doesn't bend and unbend according to its position in the water. And, if you have any doubts, you may wish to feel the "bent" stick while part of it is under water. It doesn't feel bent.

Clearly, some kind of optical illusion, in which what we see is not really so, is at work here. A mirror image is like that, too. The objects that seem to be behind the mirror are really not there at all, but somewhere else.

Let's investigate this further.

Use the penlight or flashlight with attached tube, as described in the previous section about mirrors. Darken the bathroom as much as possible. Turn on the flashlight and shine the straight beam into the water. Tilt the flashlight at various positions, from straight down to close to the water at glancing angles. You see the light beam bend sharply at the point where it enters the water. It

Light bends as it enters water.

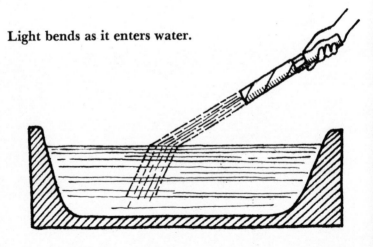

travels straight in the air and straight in the water, but at
the place where the water and air meet, the light beam
makes a sharp downward bend.

You may be bothered by what seems to be a contradiction between the way the part of a stick in water in the
tub seems to bend upward, while the part of the light
ray entering the water seems to bend downward. Notice
this difference in the drawings on the previous two pages.

This apparent contradiction is easily explained by
more careful analysis of what happens to light when it is
in water. Below, you see the straight stick AB as it really
is. The eye of an observer, above the water, receives reflected light from the bottom of the stick, B. But the
light ray from B does not travel straight as it passes from
water to air but it bends at D following the path BDC
to reach the eye.

Why objects in water seem to be higher

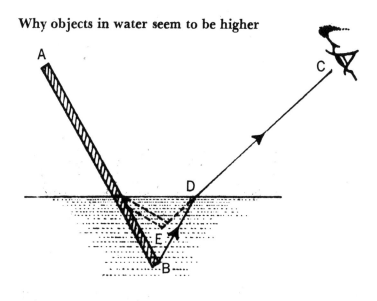

The observer has no way of knowing exactly where the light ray comes from. It enters the eye in the direction DC. To the observer the light appears to have come straight from in back of D, or from a point around E. That's where the bottom of the stick seems to be.

Notice that point E is higher than B, so the stick appears to be bent upward. Also, observe that the stick appears shorter than it really is. These two observations apply to all objects in water. The underwater portion of an object partly in water always seems to be shorter than it really is. And all objects in water seem to be closer to the surface than they really are.

Have you ever tried to spear a fish in water? If so, you may have learned that it is very difficult to do. Part of the reason is that the fish isn't where it seems to be. If you aim straight at the fish the spear will go too high. So you must allow for the change in direction of the light rays by aiming a bit lower.

There is only one position in which a very narrow parallel beam from a flashlight doesn't bend: when it is vertical, or straight down. In that position the light strikes the water at right angles and goes straight down without bending.

The bending of a light beam when it enters a transparent material (like water or glass) from another transparent material (like air) is called refraction. It is of considerable importance. The operation of all optical instruments that use lenses depends upon refraction. Human and animal sight also depend upon the refraction of light by the lens of the eye.

Much more could be said about the interesting action of light in the bathtub. But there is plenty for you to investigate by yourself. The questions and investigations suggested will help you to get started on your own.

No bending occurs at right angles.

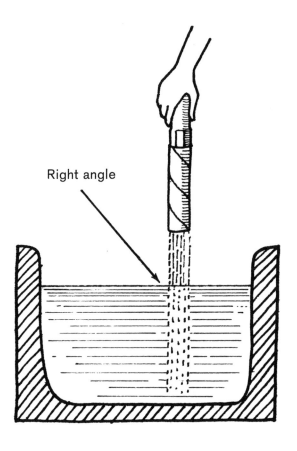

Right angle

Brain Teasers
Answers appear on page 115.

1. Look out the window on a sunny day. The window seems almost invisible. But at night, mirror reflections of objects inside the room are clearly seen in the window glass.

The reverse happens if you are standing outside in a sunny place, looking inside. The reflections are seen in the daytime and disappear at night.

How could you explain this difference?

2. Very large mirrors on the walls of a room can make it seem much larger. Why is this so?

3. When you open your eyes under water in a clear lake or pool, objects at the bottom appear blurred. But if you put on a water mask that has a clear glass front and an air chamber between it and the eyes, you can then see clearly. Can you explain why?

Investigations on Your Own

1. Hinge two thin mirrors together by taping them along one edge of each. Stand the mirrors on edge on a colored picture. Beautiful kaleidoscopic designs are observed in the mirrors.

Spread the mirrors apart and watch how the images change.

Study these mirror images and find out why they are formed.

2. Mirror images are reversals of the original objects. For example, if you cover your left eye while looking into a mirror, the image seems to cover its right eye. But if you look into a set of two mirrors placed at right angles (forming a corner) to each other, then the reversal is reversed, and all objects are seen as they normally appear.

Set up two mirrors at right angles to each other and investigate what you really look like. Do you look strange to yourself? Can you comb your hair properly while watching your corrected image?

3. Look into a mirror and watch your hand as you try to write your name on a sheet of paper. Block a direct view by placing a book between your eye and your hand. You will find that you can't write your name. Investigate this strange effect.

4. Look through a glass of water at a pencil held vertically on the other side of the glass. Move the pencil to the left, then to the right. Which way does the pencil move? Try this with the pencil close to the glass, then at arm's length. Find an explanation for what you observe.

5. Read about the refraction of light in convex and concave lenses and how it causes images to be formed. You can investigate such lenses from a pair of discarded eyeglasses. Older people tend to be farsighted, and their eyeglasses are generally convex. Nearsighted people wear concave lenses.

Magnetism 5

What is the bathtub made of? Did you ever stop to think about that? After all, it is such a simple, natural question.

There is a simple way to find out. A magnet is the key to the mystery. Any kind of magnet will do.

You probably already know that objects attracted by magnets are generally made mainly of iron. Among the familiar iron objects attracted are: paper clips, washers, nails, bolts and nuts, and parts of tools like hammers, pliers, and screwdrivers. If one of these objects is not attracted by a magnet, it is most likely made of a material other than iron.

The only other common pure metal attracted by magnets is nickel—as in a Canadian nickel (coin). In the United States nickel coin, the metal nickel is mixed with other metals to form an alloy that is not attracted by magnets.

Metals like aluminum, copper, brass, and lead are not noticeably attracted by magnets. Nor are objects made of plastics, paper, wood, cloth, rubber, glass, and almost all other materials.

Iron objects covered by paint, enamel, or similar materials will still be attracted by magnets since these coverings have no effect on magnetism. Even if an object made of iron does not look as though it is made of iron, we can still detect the iron with a magnet despite the outer covering.

When you place a magnet against the side of the bathtub you find that it is pulled toward the tub. This means that the bathtub is made either mainly of iron or of pure nickel. Since pure nickel is much more expensive than iron, it is hardly likely that this is the material used for the tub. The evidence, therefore, is strong that the tub is made of iron.

What is the bathroom sink made of? Why not see for yourself?

Why is the iron of a bathtub coated? Since you can't easily investigate the iron of the tub, an iron nail could serve as a substitute for an investigation.

Suppose you put some water in a plastic vial or dish, dropped the nail into the water, and put the vial aside. A day or so later you would find that the nail had become rusty. When you shook the vial, small brown flakes of rust might drop off into the water and the water might turn brown. If you are not content to take our word for it, try it out for yourself.

Remove the rusty water each day and replace it with clean water. Does the nail continue to rust? What happens to it after a week? a month? a year?

During the rusting of the nail, iron combines with

the gas (oxygen) that gets into the water from the air. The iron changes into a new substance called iron oxide. It happens that water speeds up the process a great deal, so that wetting the iron in any way makes it rust that much sooner.

Do all metals rust? If you are not happy with a guess, find out for yourself. Instead of the plain nail try: a galvanized iron nail, a penny (copper), a nickel (mainly a nickel alloy), a dime (silver), aluminum foil, a brass object (made of copper and zinc), a lead fishing sinker.

What would happen to a bathtub made of plain iron? You can imagine that it would rust away very quickly after water is put into the tub.

How can the rusting be prevented? Any kind of covering that keeps oxygen and water away from the iron will stop the rusting. Paint will do the trick, but it rubs off easily and is also attacked by water over a long period of time. A non-rusting metal may be plated on the iron, thereby covering it. For example, galvanized iron is iron covered with non-rusting zinc. Such plated iron could be used for tubs, but after a while any scratch deep enough to reach the iron below would cause it to rust under the scratch. Tubs could also be made of metals that resist corrosion like brass or copper. But these metals are much more expensive than iron.

The iron in most tubs is protected by a glass-like covering. At the factory, the tub is coated with a paste that contains clay and powdered stone. It is then baked at white heat until the paste becomes glassy porcelain. This coating is hard, smooth, difficult to scratch, and long-lasting, and it stops the rusting of the iron.

NORTHERN CANADA AND YOUR BATHTUB

What on earth does northern Canada have to do with your bathtub?

If you have a magnetic compass, observe that one end of the compass needle is colored differently from the other. Suppose that the north-seeking end is colored blue and the south-seeking end white. Try this. Hold the compass in a flat position and bring it near the top of the bathtub. The blue end of the compass needle turns around and points toward the tub. Now place the compass on the floor near the tub. This time, the white end of the needle turns to point toward the tub.

Try different parts of the top and bottom of the tub. The same thing always happens. All parts of the top of the tub attract the blue end of the compass needle. All parts of the bottom of the tub attract the white end.

A number of facts are needed before these actions of the compass can be understood. These facts can be obtained with some investigations using a bar-shaped magnet.

Suppose that the magnet is taped to the bottom of a small, flat plastic dish and floated in quiet water in the center of a bathtub full of water. What do you think would happen?

The dish with the magnet would turn around, vibrate slowly from side to side, and finally come to rest with the magnet pointing in a certain direction. If we turn

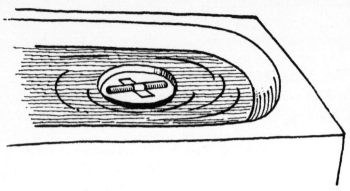

One way to make a magnetic compass

the dish a bit and let go, the dish again turns so that the magnet ends up pointing in the same direction as before. Why not try it for yourself?

Is the bar magnet in the dish pointing north? Use a regular magnetic compass to find out. Keep the compass away from the tub or sink because, as you have seen, the iron in the tub interferes with the direction-finding action of the compass. Hold the compass flat on the palm of your hand and watch the needle. The needle turns around and the blue end points in one particular direction. That direction is close to (but not exactly) north. It will be the same direction as that toward which the bar magnet in the dish points.

Many people shorten the names "north-seeking" or "south-seeking" end or pole to just "north" or "south" pole. This is fine for everyday use, but as you will soon see, this seemingly slight change causes a great deal of confusion when we get down to an explanation of what is happening. In the discussion that follows, keep in mind that the north-seeking pole of a magnet is not the same as the North Pole of the earth. The north-seeking end of a magnet is the end that happens to point approximately north, if you let it turn. The North Pole of the earth is a geographic location, the place on earth which locates the axis around which the earth turns.

To confuse "north-seeking pole" with "North Pole" would be like calling a hunting dog a bird just because the dog *pointed* toward a bird. So keep in mind during the following discussion that the phrase "north-seeking" and the word "north" refer to entirely different things.

The needle of the compass is a magnet and it spins easily because it is mounted on a sharp point. The magnet in the dish spins easily because it is floating on water. In both cases we have a magnet that is free to turn. And both turn to line up in a certain direction—almost north.

We say "almost" north because the north-seeking end of a compass needle does not point toward the *geographic* north pole in the center of the Arctic region. Instead, it points toward a place in northern Canada that is one of two *magnetic* poles of the earth. Another magnetic pole of the earth in the Antarctic attracts the south-seeking end of a compass needle.

A question arises. Why should the compass select a special place in northern Canada to point toward? Why not due east, or due west, or toward the North Pole, or toward Chicago or Buenos Aires? What force pulls it toward northern Canada?

You may know that all magnets have at least two poles, or places where the magnetism is strongest. Most rod or bar-shaped magnets have magnetic poles at their ends, although they can be manufactured with the poles in other parts of the bar.

If we take two magnets and bring their north-seeking ends close together we feel a repelling force that pushes the bars apart. The same thing happens with the south-seeking poles of the magnets. Therefore, poles that are alike repel.

On the other hand, if you hold the north-seeking end of one magnet near the south-seeking end of the other, you will feel the two magnets pull together. A north-seeking pole always attracts a south-seeking pole, and vice versa. Thus, unlike poles attract.

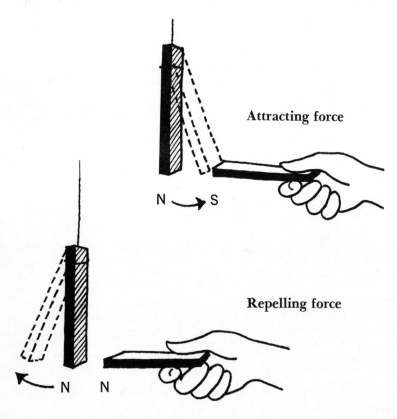

Attracting force

N ⟶ S

Repelling force

N   N

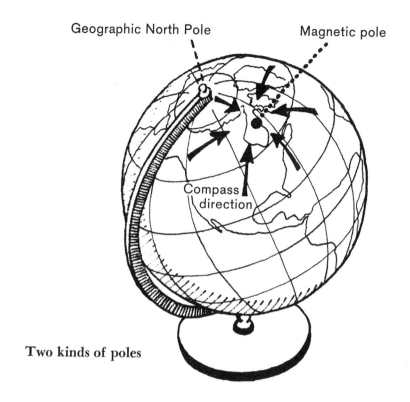

Geographic North Pole   Magnetic pole

Compass
direction

Two kinds of poles

The earth is a giant magnet. It, too, has magnetic poles, one in (or under) northern Canada, and the other in the Antarctic. These are earth-sized magnetic poles. They exert a magnetic force strong enough to be felt all over the earth. If we permit a magnet to swing freely, as happens when a magnet is placed on a floating dish or when pivoted on a sharp point, one of its magnetic poles turns toward the general direction of northern Canada while the other end swings and points in the general direction of the Antarctic.

But perhaps you sense a problem with words. Shouldn't the north-seeking pole of a magnet really be its south pole, since it is attracted to the earth's North Pole? And shouldn't the south-seeking pole of a magnet really be its north pole, since it is attracted to the earth's South Pole? Rather confusing, isn't it? How did this confusion come about?

Some five or six centuries ago when men first began to use compasses, they gave names to the ends of the compasses. The names they picked seemed natural enough. The end of the magnet that tended to point toward what they thought was the North (geographic) Pole was simply called the north pole. The other end was called a south pole. As we have seen, this was a most unfortunate choice of names.

But the original mystery remains. Why did the north end of the compass needle (the one marked blue) turn toward the bathtub when brought near the top? Why did the south end (white) point toward the tub when held near the floor?

What does the pointing of the north end of the compass needle toward the top of the tub tell us? The top of the tub must be a south pole, attracting unlike, or north, poles. The bottom of the tub attracts the south pole of the compass, so it must be a north pole.

The magnet in a floating dish and the pivoted magnet of a compass are not *completely* free to move. They are free to move around in a level circle, but they are not permitted to point up and down. If we place a compass needle in a north-south direction and also arrange it so that the ends can move up or down, as shown, then something interesting happens. In the United States, the north end of a compass needle that is free to move vertically dips quite a bit—in fact, about 60° to 70°. It acts as

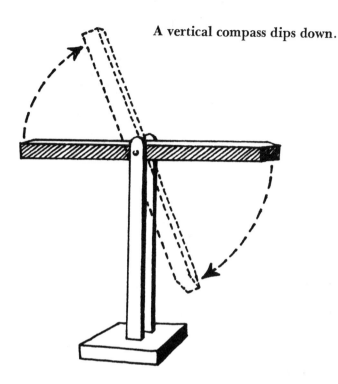

A vertical compass dips down.

though it is attracted by a magnetic pole far *below* Canada rather than by something at the surface.

The iron of the tub is a magnetic substance because the tiny grains of which it is made are each small magnets with north and south poles. And these magnetic grains of iron can turn around.

As a result, the earth's magnetic attraction for the grains of iron causes them to turn around gradually until they line up with their north-seeking ends pointing 60° to 70° downward. These north-seeking ends of many tiny grains, all pointing toward the bottom of the tub, produce a combined effect of a large north pole at the bottom. At the same time, the south poles of the tiny grains

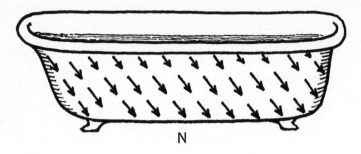

S

N

Lineup of magnetic molecules in a bathtub

of iron slant upward, creating a south pole at the top of the tub.

And so the mystery of the magnetic tub is explained.

Should iron radiators also have north poles at the bottom and south poles at the top? Of course! *Every* stationary iron object in the United States is magnetized rather rapidly by the earth so that there is a north pole at the bottom and a south pole at the top. Even an umbrella with an iron shaft, left standing for a while, develops magnetic poles in the same way. Why not test it and see for yourself?

While you are at it, test other iron objects, too. Try: a filing cabinet, refrigerator, stove, washing machine, steel door. What do you find?

Recently there has been an interesting development in geology that relates to this subject. It seems that certain rocks in the earth are found to have slight magnetic poles that were formed millions of years ago at a time when they poured out of the earth as molten lava and then cooled and hardened. But some of these rocks are actually magnetized with their north-seeking poles pointing south. This is opposite to what we would expect on the basis of the magnetic poles we observe today.

What conclusion might we draw? One possibility is that the earth's poles became reversed in the distant past. We suspect that this may have happened several times, or even many times. Of course, this raises interesting questions about the earth's structure, questions that are still being explored by scientists.

Brain Teasers
Answers appear on page 116.

1. A boy in Quito, Ecuador, on the equator, reads this book and wants to see if his bathtub is magnetized with the north pole at the bottom and south at the top.

What will he find when he tries it?

2. A girl in Tierra del Fuego, Argentina, latitude 55° south of the equator, corresponds with the boy in Quito and he tells her about his findings. She decides to test her bathtub for magnetism. What will she find?

Investigations on Your Own

1. Find out how to make the head of a nail a north pole or a south pole.

2. Find out how to make a magnet with three magnetic poles.

3. Find out how to make a magnet by using electric current.

Clocks and Tubs, Boxes and People

6

If we asked, "How much does the water in a full bath-tub weigh?" we suspect that you couldn't care less. But suppose we asked you to find out by using a clock? Now are you interested?

Get a pint jar. If you don't have such a jar use a 1-cup measuring cup and pour 2 cups into a large jar. Mark that level. It is 1 pint.

If you were a schoolboy living about a century ago, you would probably have been taught this little jingle: "A pint's a pound, the world around." The pint refers to a pint of water. According to this jingle, a pint of water weighs 1 pound. Actually, the jingle is not absolutely accurate. A pint of water really weighs 1.043 pounds, and if one wishes to be quite exact, that figure should be used. But for the kind of measurements you will be making it will be sufficiently accurate to assume that a pint of water weighs 1 pound.

Turn on the faucet in the tub so that the flow is not

too rapid, and catch the water in the pint container. Use a watch or clock with a second hand to see how much time it takes to fill the container. Suppose that it takes 10 seconds. That's ⅙ of a minute. In 1 minute, at that rate of flow, 6 pints of water, or 6 pounds, are added to the tub.

Keep the water flowing at the same rate. Open the drain to let out any water in the tub. Then close the drain and note the time at which the water begins to fill the tub. Note the time at which the tub is full (up to the overflow drain or to any mark you select). Suppose that this takes 40 minutes. Then, since the flow is 6 pounds of water a minute, the weight of water in the tub is 6 × 40, or 240 pounds.

Actually, such a small weight of water would apply only to a small tub. A tub of regular size would have perhaps 500 pounds of water. Forty minutes is a long time to wait. To speed up the process you would probably prefer to turn the faucet on full. But then you would need a bigger container to begin with, say a 1-gallon pail. One gallon is 4 quarts. One quart is 2 pints. Thus 1 gallon is 8 pints, and the water in it weighs about 8 pounds. To be more exact, it weighs 8 × 1.043, or 8.34 pounds.

Suppose that it takes 12 seconds at a faster rate of flow to fill a 1-gallon container. In exactly 1 minute, $^{60}/_{12}$ or 5 gallons of water flow into the tub. The weight of this water is about 5 × 8, or 40 pounds.

Suppose that it now takes 11 minutes to fill the tub. Then the total amount of water entering the tub is 11 × 40, or 440 pounds.

What's the point of using this clock method of weighing water? Well, just imagine the more direct approach. You might fill the tub with water, disconnect the pipes attached to the tub, pull the tub away from the wall, and use a derrick to lift it onto a great big scale that you somehow dragged into the bathroom. You would weigh the tub with water, let the water drain out, weigh the tub without water, and subtract to get the weight of the water alone. You will agree that this is hardly a practical way to find the weight of water in your bathtub.

Of course, you could take the weight of the water piecemeal by using only a pail and a bathroom scale.

Weigh a pail on a scale. Then fill the pail with water, and again weigh it. Subtract the weight of the pail and obtain the weight of the water. Then pour the water into the tub with the drain closed. Now, without a clock to help, you would have to keep doing this until the tub was filled. The total weight of water would be obtained by adding up the weights of the separate pailfuls.

Which method do you think is easier—using the clock or adding full pails of water, one by one?

If you are not sure, why not try both ways and you will soon find out.

Now let's ask another question. If you were the shape of a solid cubic box, how big a box would you be? Or, let's put it a bit differently. Suppose a hollow model is made of your body and you fill the model with sand. How large a cubic box would contain the same volume of sand—one that is 2 feet on each edge, or one 15 inches on each edge, or what? Interestingly enough, a clock can help you answer this question, too.

As you may know, the volume of a box is easily obtained by measuring length, width, and height with a ruler and multiplying all three dimensions. For example, a box 10 inches long, 10 inches wide, and 10 inches high is 10 × 10 × 10, or 1,000 cubic inches.

But how would you use a ruler to measure the width and thickness of a person? Would you take the greatest width, or the least? The ruler method of measuring volume just won't work.

Can you measure the volume of the body by filling it with water from a measuring cup? Hardly.

Can we pour your body into a box? We wouldn't recommend that at all.

But there is a simple way of replacing the volume of your body with that of water, and then measuring the volume of water in the usual way. The method is known as displacement, because you displace water by getting into it. Then the volume of displaced water can be measured.

This method works because two different things usually cannot occupy the same space at the same time. When you get into a tub of water and sink into it, the presence of your body drives away the water from the places it formerly occupied. Where can the water go? The only place is up, and so the level of water rises in the tub as your body is lowered into it. Now, all you need do to measure the volume of your body is to mark the levels of water in the tub before and after getting into it, and then measure the volume of that extra water—perhaps by the clock method.

Here is your procedure. Fill the tub with enough

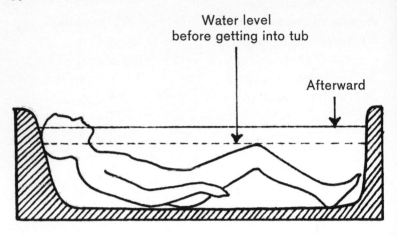

Water level
before getting into tub

Afterward

A method of finding your volume

water for you to immerse yourself almost completely. But before getting into the tub, make a temporary mark of some kind on its side in order to record the low water level. A "china marker" pencil is good for this purpose because the mark is easily rubbed off later. A piece of masking tape may also be used to mark the side of the tub. The tape may be removed when the measurement is completed.

Get into the tub and sink as far as you can, with just your nostrils and eyes out of water. Mark the side of the tub any way you can.

Now that the high and low water levels have been marked, the problem is to find out how much volume they represent. First, get out of the tub. And, of course, dry yourself. Observe that the water level is back to the first mark, the one made before you got in. The problem of finding your volume is now reduced to finding the volume of water that would occupy the space between the high and low marks on the side of the tub.

Find this volume by the clock method described earlier in the chapter. Note the time and turn on the water. As the water runs in, have it fill up a container, such as a pint or quart jar. See how long it takes for that to fill up. Then see how long it takes for the water to reach the high mark on the tub.

One young friend of ours found that his volume is 10 gallons, or 40 quarts. What do you find for yourself?

Do you have handy a carton that groceries are packed in? Perhaps one was brought home after a recent shopping trip. Take a look at it. Do you have as much volume as that box? Perhaps more, or perhaps less? How could you tell? That's not difficult to calculate if you are given this important bit of information: 1 gallon has the same volume as 231 cubic inches.

Suppose that you measure the volume of your body and find it to be exactly 10 gallons, or 2,310 cubic inches. How big a box is that? Suppose that we limit the problem by assuming that the box is a cube; that is, all sides are equal. In that case we need to find a number that when multiplied by itself three times is equal to 2,310. Or, as a mathematician would say: What is the cube root of 2,310?

Try $10 \times 10 \times 10$. That's equal to 1,000. Too little.

Try $20 \times 20 \times 20$. That's equal to 8,000. Too much.

Try $15 \times 15 \times 15$. That's equal to 3,375. Still too much.

Try $13 \times 13 \times 13$. That's equal to 2,197. Close.

Try $14 \times 14 \times 14$. That's equal to 2,744. A bit too much.

It is clear that a box about 13 inches high, 13 inches wide, and 13 inches deep has about the same volume as a person with a volume of 40 quarts. That's a box not much larger than one foot on each edge. Doesn't seem like much, does it?

Brain Teasers
Answers appear on page 117.

1. Water flows into a swimming pool 60 feet long, 25 feet wide, and 4 feet deep at a rate of 1 gallon every second. How long will it take to fill the pool?

Hints: (a) The volume in a box is calculated by multiplying the length by the width by the height. (b) One cubic foot equals 7.5 gallons.

2. Water begins to flow into a 60-gallon bathtub at the rate of 4 gallons a minute. After 5 minutes someone turns on a shower downstairs, and as a result the rate of flow drops to 2 gallons a minute. How much more time than before is required to fill the tub?

Investigations on Your Own

1. You are told that there are 2 cups to a pint, 2 pints to a quart, and 4 quarts to a gallon. This means that there are 16 cups to a gallon. Is this really so? Check this fact for yourself.

2. Does a pint of water really weigh 1.043 pounds? Try

weighing a pint of water with a scale, as accurately as you can.

3. Is a gallon really the same volume as 231 cubic inches? Prove it by actual measurement.

The Gold Crown
Mystery

7

Once upon a time—in fact, about 2,200 years ago—there lived a Greek mathematician-philosopher-scientist and amateur detective named Archimedes. Archimedes had a king named Hiero II.

The king had a gold crown, which he no doubt put on his head to impress people on important occasions. Kings being what they are, Hiero was afraid that perhaps the crown was not really made of pure gold. If so, he, a king, would be wearing an impure crown, and he would have been cheated by his crown-maker.

We can assume that a nervous king like Hiero would have been clever enough to weigh the gold before he gave it to the craftsman who made the crown. It would then be a simple matter to check the weight of the crown afterward to see if an appreciable amount of gold had been stolen. And we presume that Hiero did just that, and found that the weight was the same.

But Hiero was a smart, although suspicious, fellow. We

can just see him thinking to himself the way the crown-maker might reason: I could fool the king by removing a small portion of the gold, replacing it with an equal weight of silver, a less expensive metal, and melting both together to form an alloy. I could arrange it so that the weight of the crown would be the same as that of the original gold—and if I didn't take too much gold away, the alloy would still look like gold.

This possibility bothered Hiero. So he called in his scientific adviser, Archimedes, and delegated him to play detective and find out if any gold had been stolen in this manner.

One day Archimedes was in the bathtub thinking about the king's problem. Then, so the story goes, a method of solving the problem suddenly dawned on him. He was so excited, we are told, that he jumped out of the bathtub and darted through the streets of his city, Syracuse—without any clothes on, mind you—shouting "Eureka! Eureka!" ("I found it! I found it!")

What Archimedes had figured out was a relationship between volume and weight when an object is in a fluid such as water. This relationship enabled him to solve his problem.

Take a rubber or plastic ball, or other light object, and push it under water in the bathtub. Note how the water seems to push the ball upward. The ball is said to be buoyed up.

Release the ball. Watch it shoot up out of the water. As you can see, the upward push, or buoyancy, is strong enough to make the ball rise very rapidly.

Do the same thing again, but this time in a container

just big enough to accommodate the ball. Now note that the water level rises as the ball is pushed under the water, as shown. The ball is said to displace water. The amount of water displaced is called the displacement. This displacement is equal in volume to that of the object causing it. In other words, the volume of the object is equal to the volume of the displaced water. You will recall that we made use of this fact to measure your own volume in the preceding chapter.

An object displaces water.

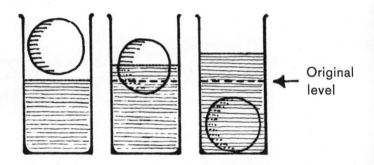

Original
level

Repeat with a larger ball (of greater volume). Now it takes much more downward force on your part to hold the ball under water. The buoyancy of the water is greater because of the greater volume, or displacement, of the ball. What Archimedes discovered, and stated in his principle, is that *buoyancy* (the upward push on an object in water) *is equal to the weight of water displaced* (pushed aside) *by the object*. For example, if the ball displaces 1 pound of water, then it is buoyed up by a 1-pound force. If it displaces 2 pounds of water, the buoyancy is 2 pounds.

Why does a rubber ball float if dropped into water? When the ball is dropped, it is pulled down by the earth's force of gravity. As it moves downward through the water, it displaces, or pushes aside, a greater and greater volume of water. And, according to Archimedes' Principle, the buoyancy increases with the increasing displacement of water. The amount of buoyancy is always equal to the weight of that displaced water. Therefore, as the ball moves downward the buoyancy increases. Finally, when the upward buoyancy equals the downward weight of the ball at a certain position, the two forces balance and the ball floats at that position.

It is possible for an object to be so heavy that even when it is completely immersed in water the buoyancy just doesn't equal the weight of the object. This would happen, for example, if the object were made of solid iron. In that case, there wouldn't be enough buoyancy to equal the total weight. Then the object couldn't float. It would be pulled downward by the unbalanced force of gravity and sink to the bottom.

THE CASE OF THE STOLEN GOLD

Now let's return to Hiero's problem, which became Archimedes' problem. How could he distinguish between pure gold and impure gold, which looks the same?

It happens that gold is a very dense substance. If equal volumes of gold and water are weighed, the gold will be found to weigh 19.3 times as much as the water. The gold is said to have a specific gravity of 19.3. Silver is dense, but not so dense as gold. It has a specific gravity of 10.5. That is, it weighs 10.5 times as much as an equal volume of water. We can also look at this in another way. Suppose that we took equal weights of water and gold. Which would have the greater volume? Since the gold is much denser than water, 19.3 times as much, it need have only 1/19.3 as much volume to have the same weight as water.

You can see that if two objects are of equal weight, the one that has less volume is denser.

If gold had been removed from Hiero's crown and replaced by the same weight of silver, the crown would weigh as much as the original gold and we couldn't tell by weighing it whether any had been stolen. But if the crown contained any silver, it would be slightly less dense than gold. It would then have a slightly larger volume than an equal weight of pure gold.

The story doesn't tell us exactly what procedure Archimedes followed. Here is one he might have employed. Imagine that Archimedes took some gold from the original batch from which the crown had supposedly been made and fashioned a piece that weighed exactly the same as the crown. He would have reasoned that if the crown was made of pure gold, then the crown and the equal weight of pure gold would have exactly the same volume or displacement of water. But if the volume or displacement of the crown was greater, Archimedes would be sure that its gold had been mixed with a less dense metal, such as silver.

Whatever procedure Archimedes followed, he found that the crown did actually have a lower density than pure gold. It was therefore clear that the gold had been tampered with by the king's crown-maker.

We can't help but feel sorry for the poor craftsman who came to an unhappy end by virtue of Archimedes' detective work. But you must admit that Archimedes, in addition to his many other achievements, could lay claim to the honor of being the first scientific detective in history.

THE WATER DROP PUZZLE

No doubt you are inspired by Archimedes' example to do likewise. So, just for practice, we present a little mystery for you in the form of a science puzzle.

You are given:

    1 bathtub with water
    1 vial, 1 inch in diameter
    several nickels (weight of each nickel: 5 grams)
    1 dropper
    1 china marker or grease pencil

The problem: Use these materials—and no others—to find the weight of a drop of water.

First think about the problem and try to figure out a procedure of your own. Then check your reasoning with the one suggested below.

After putting the vial in the water, add the nickels, one at a time, until the vial floats upright. Then add one more nickel. If necessary, shift the positions of the nickels so that the vial is vertical.

Mark the water line on the outside of the vial with the china marker.

Remove one nickel. The vial floats higher out of the water.

Now add drops of water with the dropper until the vial sinks to the original level, before the nickel was removed. Count the number of drops added.

According to Archimedes' Principle, buoyancy depends only on the displacement of water. If the vial is floating at the same level at two different times, the displacement and buoyancy must be the same. Therefore the weight buoyed up in both cases is the same. In other words, we have replaced the weight of a nickel with an equal weight of drops of water.

It happens that the United States Mint manufactures nickels that weigh 5 grams. (A gram is about $\frac{1}{28}$ of an ounce.) Suppose that 50 drops of water were required to restore the floating level of the vial. Then we know that 50 drops weigh the same as one nickel, or 5 grams. Then 1 drop of water weighs $\frac{5}{50}$, or $\frac{1}{10}$ of a gram. Easy, isn't it?

Brain Teasers
Answers appear on page 118.

1. Why does a life preserver enable a person to keep his head above water?

2. Some kerosene is poured into a container of water and floats on top of it. A piece of wax is then dropped in. It

is observed to float at the boundary between the kerosene and the water. Can you explain why?

3. Archimedes was once given the problem by his king of measuring an elephant's weight in gold. There were no scales available to measure such a heavy weight. Can you figure out how Archimedes solved the problem in a rather simple way?

Investigations on Your Own

1. Can you prove that Archimedes' Principle for a floating object is true? Figure out a way to do this.

Will it suffice to try one object? Or should you try many?

2. Here is a procedure to weigh yourself in the bathtub.

Mark the level of water in the bathtub when you are out of it, and again when you are floating in it, with just the tip of your nose out of the water. Measure the volume of displaced water by any of the methods described in Chapter 6.

Now you need to have this information: Water weighs 62.5 pounds per cubic foot.

Suppose that you displace 2 cubic feet of water. Since 1 cubic foot of water weighs 62.5 pounds, you displace 2 × 62.5, or 125 pounds of water. That is your weight, because it is the buoyancy that the displaced water exerts on you when you are floating.

If you measure your volume in gallons you will also need to use one of the following facts:

$$1 \text{ gallon} = 231 \text{ cubic inches}$$
$$1 \text{ cubic foot} = 7.5 \text{ gallons}$$

Hot and Cold 8

The next time you are about to take a bath wait a bit to turn on the water. Get into the tub and try to sit down without any water. Brrr . . . Can you imagine how cold it would feel?

Is the tub itself cold? Think a minute. If the tub were actually colder than the air and other objects nearby, then it would gradually be warmed by them and soon reach the same temperature.

The tub *is* as warm as its surroundings. Test it with a thermometer. Keep the thermometer in the room for about five minutes or so, time enough for it to reach the temperature of the room. What is the temperature? Rest the thermometer on the bottom of the empty bathtub. Bring the bulb of the thermometer in contact with the tub. Wait five minutes and read the temperature. Does it change?

If the empty tub is no colder than anything else in the bathroom, why should it *feel* so cold?

Our bodies are not the best devices for sensing temperature. What the body senses is its gain or loss of heat.

If it loses heat very rapidly, and the skin is thereby cooled off very rapidly, the body feels cold. If the body gains heat very rapidly, it feels hot.

You are warm-blooded, which means that your body normally maintains a constant temperature, about 98.6° Fahrenheit. The temperature of a comfortable room is about 68° to 72°. Since your body is about 30° warmer than the surroundings in a comfortable room, you must lose heat constantly to the surroundings.

If so, why is a room at 70° more comfortable than one at 90°? To exist, you must burn up food, and this always produces heat. But if the heat were permitted to accumulate inside your body, its temperature would rise steadily. At a body temperature of 105° one would be in serious trouble. Since death usually occurs if a person's temperature is 110° even for a short time, the body must constantly lose some of its heat to the surroundings if it is to survive.

A room at 70° is comfortable because at that temperature the proper rate of flow of heat out of the human body just about equals the rate at which new heat is normally produced by the burning of food.

But what happens if you are in a hot sauna room with the air at 170°? How could one even exist at that temperature? The pores of your sweat glands open up and large quantities of sweat pour out onto the skin. The liquid then rapidly evaporates into the air. This evaporation cools the body, at least enough to survive at 170° for about 15 to 30 minutes. Without this cooling effect of evaporation, no man could survive temperatures much above 95°.

You can easily observe the cooling effect of evaporation by your own investigations. Wet the back of your hand and let the water evaporate. Does it feel cooler?

Or try this. Wrap a small piece of cotton around the bulb of a thermometer. Wet it with water at room temperature. Watch the thermometer as the water evaporates from the cotton. The temperature may drop 10° or 20°, or even more. After all the water has evaporated, the temperature rises to normal because there no longer is any cooling effect.

Here is another simple investigation you can perform right in the bathtub. Let's suppose that you proceeded normally with your bath instead of being sidetracked to test properties of heat. You fill the bathtub with warm water, get in, sit down, splash around, and perhaps wash a bit. Now, you are ready to get out. You stand up, reach for the towel, and quickly dry yourself. But wait. Suppose that on one occasion you do not reach for the towel right away, but just stand there a minute or two to see (or feel) what happens.

But don't wait too long. In a short while you are shivering with cold. Why? Evaporation from your wet body is cooling you very rapidly.

We have seen how man controls the temperature of his body when it is very warm. But how does he manage when the temperature drops and it turns very cold? At such low temperatures the rate of flow of heat out of the body is greater than at 70°. The body tends to cool off too rapidly, and to drop below its proper operating temperature of 98.6°. This situation is a serious threat. The body can't permit the temperature to drop for long without harm. There are two ways to solve this problem. Either the body produces more heat by burning up more food, or else it finds some way of reducing the heat loss.

Warm-blooded animals have a number of ways of reducing heat loss in cold weather. Some animals grow more fur as the winter approaches. Some birds puff up their feathers to make temporary thick coats that trap air around their bodies. This serves to keep the body heat from going out into the air. Other animals solve the problem by curling up in as round a shape as possible and going off into the deep sleep of hibernation. The round shape of a ball is the most compact and has the least surface exposed to the cold outside. This results in a lower rate of heat loss.

Hibernation is also accompanied by a sharp drop in body temperature, bringing it near the temperature of the surroundings. This greatly reduces heat loss. Finally, the body stops all conscious activity and motion, thereby reducing its need for energy. As a result, the limited food supply stored in the body is sufficient for production of heat during the long, cold months ahead.

Human beings have their own special ways of keeping body heat from being lost in cold weather. We build houses and heat them, thus creating our own comfortable 70° environment. When we go outside, we bundle ourselves in clothing that keeps us warm by reducing the rate at which heat leaves our bodies.

What kind of material should we use for clothing? How about cloth made from steel wire? It would have some advantages—strength and durability, for example. Ah! But those disadvantages! One, for example, would be the sensation that resembles sitting down in the dry bathtub. Steel clothing would feel cold at 70°, very cold at 60°, and unbearably cold at 50°.

Now we have arrived at our original problem. Why is the sensation of sitting down without clothes on in a bathtub so different from sitting down on a bed? Both the bathtub and the bed are at room temperature, about 70°. But one feels cold and the other feels just right. Obviously, there must be some difference in the way the bathtub drains heat out of the body as compared with the way the cloth of the sheet on the bed does.

Recall from Chapter 5 that the bathtub is made of iron covered with a thin layer of porcelain. Iron, and metals in general, are good conductors of heat; that is, they allow heat to travel through them rather easily. On the other hand, cotton and wool are poor conductors of heat, or insulators. They tend to block the flow of heat.

The tub feels cold because the iron rapidly conducts heat from the body surface into the bathtub. The cloth and wool of the bedding do not feel cold because they do not permit rapid flow of heat from the body into the bed.

Try this. Place a metal frying pan on one burner of a stove and a glass baking dish on another. Put a few drops of water into each. Turn on the burners at the same time and make the heat low. In which container does the water boil first? You will find that it boils first in the metal one, because the heat is conducted through the metal much more rapidly than through the glass. The glass of the baking dish is a relatively poor conductor and the inside heats up much more slowly.

Air is a very poor conductor of heat so long as it does not move about. The motion of air helps carry heat from place to place, as you may observe by holding your hand above a candle. Thus fluffy materials with spaces that trap air are excellent for stopping the flow of heat and are said to be good insulators. A picnic soda cooler, for example, might be made of styrofoam, a foam plastic that contains a large number of tiny air spaces. Cold soda put into this kind of cooler remains at low temperatures for a long time because heat from the outside comes in very slowly. Rock wool, glass wool, or asbestos materials, also filled mainly with trapped air, are used to insulate houses by keeping heat inside during the winter and outside during the summer.

On the other hand, metals are used for such things as pots and radiators where we want heat to be conducted through the material rapidly.

Test various materials in the bathroom for conduction of heat by touching them with your hand. Touch a wooden door or cabinet, a metal radiator, a doorknob. Touch a tile wall, a tile floor, a glass mirror, a plaster wall. Touch a dry towel, a blanket, a wad of paper. Which of these materials feel cold? These are the good conductors of heat, as indicated by the fact that the body loses heat rapidly where it touches these materials. Which do not feel cold? These are the insulating materials that reduce the flow of heat from the body surface.

EXPLAINING HEAT

All of these facts about heat have probably raised some questions in your mind. Why can heat pass through solid metal? Why does evaporation cause cooling?

Over the years scientists have gradually worked out a theory that accounts very nicely for the facts. The theory is based on the idea of molecules, the extremely tiny particles of which all materials are made. These molecules are in motion, even in a solid—banging into each other constantly. Yet they are kept in place in the solid by strong forces of attraction from the surrounding molecules.

The faster the molecules in a solid move, the greater the temperature of the solid. In other words, *heat is due to the motion of molecules*. The same fact applies to liquids and gases except that the molecules are freer to wander about, more so in gases than in liquids.

How can heat pass through a solid material like the metal in a pot? The explanation is not so mysterious when you consider that heat is a form of motion, or energy, not a material like water or air. It is the motion of molecules that passes through the solid.

Consider what happens in the case of food in a pan placed on the stove. The motion of molecules in the hot burning gas or in the hot electric coil is very much faster than normal. In fact, that's why it is hot. These fast-moving molecules bang into the molecules of metal on the underside of the pan and set them into rapid motion. These, in turn, bang into the molecules above and make them move more rapidly, too. So, molecule by molecule, the rapid vibrating motion is transmitted through the metal to the food in the pan.

Why do water and other liquids cool when they evaporate? Liquids differ from solids in that the vibrating molecules have broken away from each other and move about in the substance. The attractive force between molecules is no longer sufficient to keep them tied to one position, as is the case in solids. But there is enough attractive force between molecules in a liquid to keep them together in one mass at the bottom of the container.

As the molecules wander about in the liquid, they bump into each other; because of their high speed, we might say that they bombard each other. Occasionally, a molecule near the surface will be given enough speed by one of these bumps to jump out into the air above the liquid. Will it be able to escape the attractive force of its neighbors below? That depends upon how fast it goes. Some will be moving fast enough to escape completely and wander off as a gas, or vapor. These molecules evaporate.

Note that the fastest molecules are the ones that leave during evaporation. Which ones are left behind? The slower ones, of course. But slower molecules mean lower temperatures. So you can see that the water will become cool. If that evaporating water happens to be on your bare skin, you will then feel quite cold.

The molecular theory of heat that we have described is about a century and a half old. Since its beginning, thousands of scientists have tested the theory in hundreds of different ways. Now there is little doubt about its truth, and the molecular theory of heat is accepted by all scientists as true.

Brain Teasers
Answers appear on page 119.

1. Which cools off more rapidly—a bathtub full of hot water, or a glassful?
   Explain your answer.

2. Can you think of three ways to increase evaporation of a liquid? Explain why each method helps evaporation.

3. Why do you feel warmer when the day is humid than when it is dry?

Investigations on Your Own

1. Find out how a refrigerator makes use of the cooling effect of evaporation.

2. Design and build a small box that will keep one ice cube from completely melting in 10 hours.

Bubbles

9

Did you ever take a bubble bath? No? Then you should try one.

Special sudsing solutions and powders are sold for making baths bubbly. If you already have such a bubble bath material, follow the directions on the package and make a mountain of bubbles in the bathtub. If you don't have any bubble bath solution, make your own with a teaspoonful of dishwashing detergent. Have fun! But you can't enjoy the bubble bath forever. There comes a time when it's more interesting to be a scientist.

Look at the bubbles that form. Are they large or small? round or box-shaped? light or heavy? Do they last a long time, or disappear rapidly?

What are bubbles? How do they form?

Begin the investigation of these questions by "floating" a small paper clip in water in a quiet bathtub (or bowl). That's right. We said "floating" a paper clip in water. But a paper clip is made of metal. How can it "float"?

"Floating" a paper clip on water

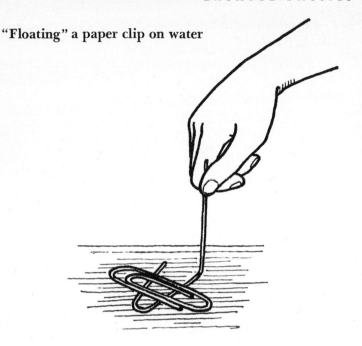

Bend a clip to make a holder, as shown. Place a small paper clip on it, as shown. Gently lower the clip flat onto the water in the bathtub or bowl. If you do this carefully, the paper clip will stay on top of the water as the holder goes below the surface.

Now try it at a slight tilt. This time the metal clip plunges to the bottom, as you expected it to. Something held up the first clip, but what?

In Chapter 8 you learned that all substances are made of tiny particles called molecules. These molecules attract each other, if very close together. In solids, the attraction is so strong that the molecules stay together, and it takes a strong force to pull them apart and break the material.

In liquids, the attraction is not so strong, but it is still there and quite noticeable. One good way to show this is to dip a pencil in water and lift it out. At the bottom, clinging to the pencil and apparently defying the law of gravity, is a drop of water. It seems to be attracted to the pencil by some kind of force. The force is that of attraction between the molecules of the water and those of the pencil.

Hold the pencil just above a piece of waxed paper and shake it to release the drop of water. Notice how perfectly round the drop is around the outer edge. And notice, too, how it stands up in the center, quite a bit above the waxed paper. Obviously, there is some kind of attraction inside the drop of water that pulls all parts of it together. The attractive force of the molecules for each other causes the round shape of the drop by pulling the molecules at the outer surface closer to the center. This force is known as surface tension. It causes the molecules at the surface of a liquid to be pulled closer to the inner molecules. As a result, the surface acts like a film that pulls the mass together.

Now you see why we put quotation marks around "floating" earlier. The paper clip does not stay on top of the water because of the ordinary buoyancy such as a life preserver provides. It stays up only because it is too light to break through the surface film caused by the attractive forces of the water molecules.

Look closely at the water near the paper clip as it rests on the surface. Observe how the water is dented slightly under the clip. It almost looks as though a thin flexible sheet covers the water surface and holds up the clip. Actually, there is no sheet at all. It is just the surface tension that keeps the lightweight clip from breaking through.

Many other light objects made of materials that normally sink can be supported in a similar way. Try a piece of aluminum foil; a berry basket with the bottom full of holes; a piece of thin metal screen, also full of holes. All of these can be made to stay up on the water if placed gently on the surface.

A number of insects make use of surface tension to hold them up as they skim across the water in ponds and streams. They are light enough actually to "walk" on the water.

Bubbles form in a liquid because of surface tension. To understand how this happens, try making some bubbles by letting water run out rapidly from the faucet into water in the bathtub. A small cloud of bubbles forms around the place where the water is churned up. But these bubbles don't last very long. They burst very quickly. If you shut off the water the bubbles usually disappear in a few seconds.

As the water falls through the air it mixes with air and carries some along with it. Then it plunges into the water in the bathtub carrying globs of air with it. These globs of air are momentarily carried below the surface and are pushed sidewards by the falling water above. Then they rise to the surface a short distance from the spot where the water is falling. As the glob of air rises it stretches the surface film and may not break through because of the surface tension. So a bubble is formed—a glob of air with a thin film of water molecules covering it.

If you watch closely as the water falls, you will observe that these bubbles in plain water break after just a second or so and new bubbles form from underneath. But just put a small amount of detergent or soap in the water and the bubbles suddenly last a long time. Why the difference?

Try this. Get a paper clip to stay on the surface of water in a bowl. Then add a drop of detergent (or soap solution, or bubblebath solution) to the water several inches from the drop. After a short time the paper clip will suddenly sink by itself. This happens because the detergent gradually dissolves in the water and weakens the surface tension to the point where it is no longer strong enough to hold up the clip.

Here is another way to show that detergents and soaps weaken surface tension. Let a drop of detergent or a flake of soap fall between two floating matches placed about a half inch apart in a bowl of water. The matches fly apart as though pulled by something. In fact, they *are* pulled. The detergent weakens the surface tension of the water between the matches. The surface tension on the outer sides of the matches is then greater than that between them and pulls the matches apart.

An insect known as Stenus not only walks on water by making use of surface tension but also uses that force to propel itself. The insect has a projection touching the water at its rear and a liquid oozes out that weakens the surface tension. The stronger surface tension in front then pulls the insect forward. To stop moving, all the insect does is to stop touching the water with its projection or stop the liquid from flowing out.

Well, now we have established that plain water has a greater surface tension than water with dissolved detergent or soap. Picture the problems of a glob of air trapped on all sides by a thin layer of water—in other words, a bubble. If the surface tension is strong, as is the case with pure water, the outer layer of water pulls inward quite forcefully and squeezes the air inside. The compressed air then tends to burst through the film at any weak point, breaking the bubble.

But if the surface tension is weak, the surface film can be more easily extended by the air. There is less tendency for the air to break through. So the bubble tends to last longer.

Small bubbles, or froth, may last a long time in detergent solutions, sometimes too long, in fact. As the solution works its way down the drain into a cesspool or a sewer, the bubbly froth that forms may remain for a long time. It may clog cesspools, septic tanks, or sewage treatment plants. It also tends to spoil bacterial action that is important for purification of water. Large mounds of such foam often appear in rivers due to pollution from household detergents.

The problem has become so severe in recent years that many detergent manufacturers have been forced to reduce the sudsing action of their cleaners, which, by the way, has nothing to do with the ability to clean. The only reason detergents are made sudsy is that advertisements have led people to think that sudsiness has something to do with cleansing ability. Actually the cleansing ability of soaps and detergents is due to the fact that the detergent helps the water wet food particles and other greasy substances that are normally not wet by water. The detergent molecule has two ends, with one end tending to stick to water while the other tends to stick to oils and greases. The detergent molecule thus acts as a kind of molecular bridge that enables the water and oily substances to stick together. As a result, water with dissolved soap or detergent can also dissolve oily substances and thereby remove them from pots, dishes, hands, and clothing.

The forces between molecules that give rise to surface tension and bubbles play an important part in many other events. For example, a duck swimming in water keeps itself dry by means of a layer of oil on its feathers. Water does not wet (stick to) an oily surface because the force of attraction between oil molecules and water molecules is smaller than the attraction of water to itself. But if the poor duck should happen to settle on water with too much soap or detergent in it, the attraction of the molecules of oil on its feathers for molecules of detergent in the water will form a molecular bridge between the oil and water, and the duck will get all wet. The added weight of the water sticking to the bird's feathers may make it sink and drown.

The same thing would happen to a water bug that walks on water. It would also sink in water with sufficient detergent.

So you see where our bubbles lead us—to waterlogged ducks and bugs. We end up, as is often the case, quite far afield. That is one of the things that make the study of science so very interesting.

Brain Teasers
Answers appear on page 120.

1. You blow a bubble with a pipe and then remove your mouth while the bubble is still attached to the pipe. What will happen to the bubble?

2. Suppose that you fill a narrow test tube with water until the surface is exactly level with the top of the test tube. What will happen to the water when you gently drop in a paper clip?

Investigations on Your Own

1. Surface tension can be measured directly by measuring the force required to lift a light, flat square or disk from the surface of the liquid. The force required to pull the square or disk away from the liquid may be measured with an accurate balance. Such a balance can be made with an 18-inch piece of coat hanger wire. Make a slight bend at its center and suspend the wire from the center with a piece of nylon thread so that it swings freely. Paper clips, or similar small objects, may be used as weights on one end of the wire to lift up the square or disk suspended from the other end.

Use such a device to compare the surface tensions of different liquids. Also find out what effect dissolving salt, sugar, and other substances has on the surface tension of water.

2. Make big bubbles with special bubble solutions sold for this purpose in toy stores. Or, you can make your own by dissolving different kinds of detergents in water. Soap solutions mixed with glycerine also make an excellent bubble material.

No doubt you are familiar with the use of pipes to make bubbles. A hole or holes in a sheet of metal or plastic can also serve as a bubble-maker. For example, a piece of large mesh screen (at least ½-inch square) or chicken wire works nicely. Just dip it into the bubble solution and wave it back and forth to generate bubbles.

Air Pressure

10

Do you suppose that a fish swimming in the ocean is aware that there is water around it? Do you think that a dog is aware that it walks around at the bottom of an ocean of air?

"Familiarity breeds contempt"—or at least lack of awareness. The fish, born in the water and living in it every moment of its life, no doubt is unaware of the water around it and has no sensation of the pressure of water caused by the weight above it. So, too, is the dog unaware that there is air all around it and that there is considerable air pressure on its body. You would be unaware of it, too, except for the fact that you may have been told about it or have read about it.

It requires some special occurrence to reveal the presence of air around us. It may move rapidly, as when a wind blows against us. Or a cloud may form and become visible. But perhaps the best way to become aware of the presence of air is to see how the weight of the air above causes pressure on objects below.

90

Take a plastic tumbler or other container and push it completely under water in the bathtub. Wait until it fills with water. Then turn it upside down. Slowly pull the tumbler up. Surprise! The water rises with the tumbler until it is much higher than the water in the tub!

"Lifting" water out of the bathtub

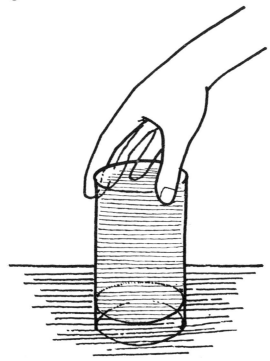

There seems to be nothing holding up the water. But something must be, or it would fall. What can the force be?

The ocean of air above us is about 100 miles deep. Although the air in this ocean seems to us to be weightless, nevertheless it does have some weight. And at the bottom of the 100-mile depth of air ocean, the weight of air is considerable. As a result, the air pressure on all objects at the surface of the earth is considerable—about 15 pounds for every square inch. Your bathtub is no exception; air presses down on the surface of water in the bathtub, as well as on everything else.

When you lift the upside-down tumbler, the water in it begins to fall because it is pulled by the earth's force of gravity. But it doesn't get very far. To understand why, imagine that the water does actually drop a bit, as shown by line A. What would be in the space above the dotted line? Certainly there is no air, and, therefore,

How air pressure holds up water

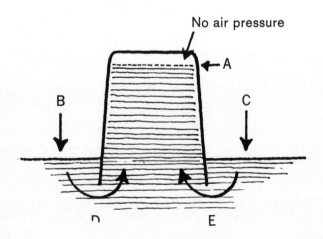

no pressure. In other words, the space above the dotted line would have no air pressure.

Now observe the arrows at B and C. They show the air pressure pressing downward on the water's surface. The water below is squeezed by the air pressure above it, and is also under pressure. The water is therefore pushed into any empty space that is available. As a result, any water in the upside-down tumbler that begins to fall is pushed back into the space that might form in the tumbler, as shown by arrows D and E.

Actually, the water in the tumbler never really drops far enough for you to notice. Air pressure immediately forces the water back up into the tumbler and keeps it there as you lift the tumbler.

If the water can be supported by air pressure in an inverted tumbler 6 inches high, will it stay up in a container 12 inches high? Two feet high? Ten feet high? Fifty feet high? If you try it out with the tallest container you can find around the house, you will find that the water stays up.

But there is a limit to the height of water that can be raised in this way. Water has weight, very much more than air, volume for volume. In fact, water weighs about 800 times as much as air for the same volume. As a result of its weight, water also exerts pressure beneath it, as does air. It happens that at a depth of 34 feet, water exerts a pressure of 15 pounds per square inch, the same as that of regular air pressure. So a column of water 34 feet high would exactly balance the upward push resulting from air pressure in a closed container. As you can see, the water could rise no higher than 34 feet.

Imagine a long, upside-down "tumbler" about 50 feet high being pulled up out of water, as shown on the facing page. When the closed part of the "tumbler" gets to a height of 34 feet above the water level, the water inside no longer rises. Instead it remains at the 34-foot level, even though the rest of the tumbler is still being lifted. As we continue to lift, a region of emptiness, sometimes called a vacuum, develops above the water level in the tall container.

What would happen to the water inside a 50-foot "tumbler" if the outside air pressure were to become less for some reason? The air pressure could no longer hold up 34 feet of water, and the water level would drop until the pressures were again in balance.

Suppose that the outside air pressure increased. It could then hold up more than 34 feet of water, and the level of water in the container would rise.

What we have described is a barometer that could be used to measure air pressure. In this case a column of water is used to balance the air pressure. The air pressure is measured by the height of the column of water it can support.

A water barometer like this was actually made by Otto von Guericke several centuries ago. Instead of a "tumbler" he used a wide glass tube more than 34 feet high, closed at the top and filled with water and sticking out of the roof of his house. The bottom of the tube rested in a container of water. Von Guericke constructed his barometer so that the water level in the upper part of the tube was visible to the townspeople, and they could watch a float on the water rise and fall as the air pressure changed. If the float in von Guericke's water barometer

A water barometer

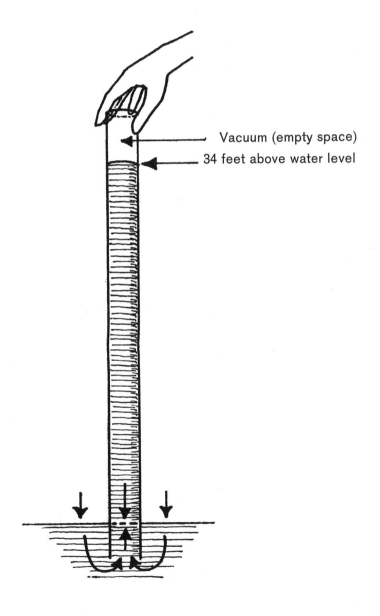

Vacuum (empty space)

34 feet above water level

went down inside the house the townspeople knew that the air pressure was lessening and poor weather was likely to arrive. On the other hand, if the float rose in the tube and came out of the house, this indicated the likelihood of good weather.

Why does a change in air pressure signal a probable change in the weather? It happens that the warm, moist air that generally brings poor weather is lighter than the cool, dry air that generally brings good weather. So, the air pressure lessens as poor weather approaches and increases with the coming of good weather.

A barometer is certainly a useful device. But a tube more than 34 feet high and almost filled with water is clearly very inconvenient to use. We can shorten the tube considerably by using mercury, a liquid metal that is 13.6 times as dense as water. A barometer containing mercury can produce the same pressure at the bottom of the tube if it is $1/13.6 \times 34$ feet, or 2½ feet, or 30 inches high. This is a much more convenient height than 34 feet. Thus, for practical purposes mercury is used instead of water to fill barometer tubes. The arrangement looks just like the water barometer shown on page 95, except that it is much smaller and no hand is required to lift the tube. It is supported in position in some suitable manner.

PUMPS AND BREATHING

Perhaps you have used a pump to blow up a bicycle tire. If so, you know that by pushing down on the handle you force air into the tire. When you pull up, the pump fills with air, in preparation for the next downward push.

Do you realize that you have a somewhat similar pumping mechanism in your body, one that works constantly day and night, whether you are asleep or awake? We refer to the process of breathing, so essential to your existence.

The similarity of your breathing apparatus to a pump is made clearer by actually using it as such. Just put a soda straw in your mouth and drink some soda from a bottle. The liquid rises in the straw and enters your mouth. Doesn't it remind you of water rising above its level when an inverted tumbler is lifted?

What makes the soda water rise? Air pressure outside pushed the soda water up, just as it pushed the water up into the tumbler in the bathtub. But the soda water wouldn't rise unless the air pressure inside your body was somewhat less than that outside. How did the air pressure decrease?

The upper part of your body, around the chest, contains two flexible containers of air, the lungs. You pump air into these containers in a simple way, just by increasing the space available inside the chest cavity. The air in the lungs then expands into the greater space and its pressure drops. Air outside, at a greater pressure, then pushes its way into the lungs through the mouth or nose. If the mouth is connected to a straw, and the end of the straw is in liquid, then the outside air pressure will push the liquid up into the low pressure area inside the body. In effect, you "pump" the liquid up to a higher place.

How does the body increase the space available? When we breathe in, the diaphragm, a muscle across the abdo-

Inhaling

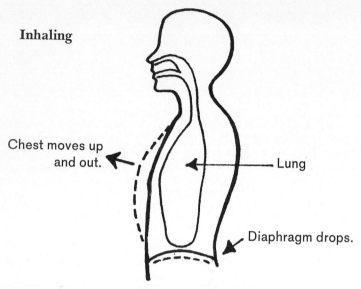

Chest moves up and out.

Lung

Diaphragm drops.

men, moves downward, enlarging the chest cavity and expanding the lungs. Air pressure in the lungs drops, and the air outside at higher pressure tends to rush in.

This action is supplemented by expansion of the chest. The bones around the chest, the ribs, are pulled outward by special chest muscles and thereby expand the body space. Again, the air outside rushes into the region of reduced pressure inside the lungs.

Breathing out is simply the reverse action. The diaphragm pushes up and the ribs are pulled inward, which makes less room available in the lungs. This squeezes the air inside the lungs, increases the pressure, and pushes some air out through the nostrils or mouth.

Observe it for yourself. Feel your abdomen move out as you breathe in. When the abdomen moves out, this indicates that the diaphragm is moving down to make more room inside.

You breathe out by contracting the space inside the body. This is accomplished by the diaphragm and chest muscles. The air inside the lungs is squeezed, pressure inside is increased and the higher pressure air moves out of the body.

Now breathe hard. This time your chest heaves violently at the same time that your abdomen moves.

How much air can you breathe? It's easy to find out. Fill a container with water, put it under the surface of the filled bathtub (or sink), and turn it upside down. Let the container float at its own level. Steady it with one hand. Insert a rubber tube into the open bottom of the container, as shown. Put the other end of the tube in your mouth and breathe out one normal breath. How much air goes into the container? That's the volume of one normal breath.

Measuring a breath

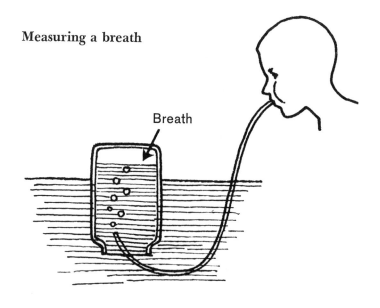

Breath

Now start over again with a container full of water. Put the tube into your mouth and breathe out one deep breath. You can push out all the water in a quart container. Try it with a 2-quart container or a gallon. What is the most you can breathe out in one breath?

Brain Teasers
Answers appear on page 121.

1. The Cartesian Diver is an interesting device, used as a kind of magic trick in which a "diver" that just barely floats in water can be made to go up and down at will. The magician makes the diver go down by pressing down-

Cartesian diver

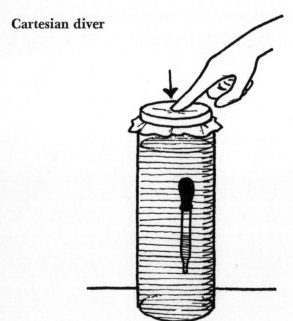

ward on the stopper (or flexible rubber sheet) at the top. When he releases the pressure the diver rises.

Explain how it works.

2. A teacher boiled some water in a clean gallon tin can. Then he shut off the heat, sealed the opening very tightly, and set the can on an asbestos pad on the table. In a short while the sides of the can began to crumple inward. This continued slowly until the can was severely crushed.

Why did this happen?

Investigations on Your Own

1. Make a Cartesian Diver like the one shown on page 100. A partly filled, barely floating medicine dropper can serve as the diver.

Study the operation of the diver. Observe the action of the water in the dropper at the moments when the rubber sheet is pressed or released.

2. Fill a long rubber or plastic tube with water. Place one end in water in a bathtub and the other end in an empty pail on the floor. The water from the bathtub flows up over the edge of the tub and into the pail without any expenditure of energy on your part.

Such an arrangement is called a siphon.

Be sure to lift the pail higher than the level of water in the tub before it overflows. Now the water flows out of the pail back into the tub.

Investigate this interesting action and find out how it works.

Forces and Motion 11

Place an empty metal or plastic bowl or pan with a rounded bottom on the surface of water in the tub. Give the bowl a spin and then let go. For how long does it continue spinning?

Quite a long time, you will agree. It certainly wouldn't spin so long on a solid table.

Now try this: Place the floating bowl at one end of the tub and give it a gentle push toward the other end. Are you surprised at the way it coasts across the water at a steady speed? That wouldn't happen if you tried to push it across the floor. Such a gentle push on the floor would do no more than make the bowl wobble a bit.

Why does the bowl move more easily on water than on a solid surface?

FRICTION

Suppose that the bowl rests on the solid surface of a table. The weight of the bowl pulls the bowl close to the table. Tiny roughnesses in both the bowl and the table then interlock a bit. When you push the bowl these interlocking roughnesses grip each other. To make the bowl move along the table you must push with enough force to overcome the effect of the roughness. This force that must be applied before an object moves freely across another surface is called friction.

From this explanation you can see that one way to reduce friction is to make the surfaces smoother. And what could be smoother than a liquid that flows easily around a solid? When the solid material is in contact with a liquid, there are no longer any interlocking solid parts. The liquid simply gives way when pushed and flows around the material of the bowl (or other object). The action of a liquid in this respect is known as lubrication, and a liquid used in this manner is said to be a lubricant.

Low friction because of lubrication is the main reason that a high proportion of home accidents occur in bathtubs. To see why, first consider one reason why we wear shoes when walking. The feet must push back against the floor to make us move forward. To help the feet grip the floor, we use high-friction leather and rubber on the soles of our shoes.

In the bathtub, friction is greatly reduced by the combination of smooth skin on the soles of the feet, a very smooth tub, and a lubricant (water) between them. As a result, the useful kind of friction people need for walking is greatly reduced. Normal motions may then cause slipping because friction is too low.

Many bathtubs have rough strips on the bottom to increase friction. No doubt in some future day bathtubs will be made with special surfaces that increase friction sufficiently to prevent slipping.

Ice-skating is another interesting example of the lubricating action of water. When the sharp blade of a skate presses against the surface of the ice, some of it under the blade melts. Then the blade is lubricated by the liquid and glides with very little friction, the way the bowl in the bathtub moves across the water.

If you watch the path of the blade right behind the skater you can actually see the liquid rapidly refreeze, generally leaving a visible mark.

Oil is the most widely used lubricant in machinery. This liquid separates metal parts that would otherwise be in contact and rub with a great deal of friction. When there is contact only between metal and oil, the friction is very much less than for metal against metal, and the parts slide past each other quite easily.

Some car drivers are not aware of how important it is that all essential parts of the car be constantly lubricated. Occasionally oil in an engine may leak out, or the oil pump may not work properly and fail to pump oil to places where friction needs to be reduced. A red light on the dashboard generally lights up to let the driver know when oil pressure is low and oil is not reaching vital parts of the engine. If the car continues to be driven for even a few minutes, the engine may be completely ruined by the heat caused by the rubbing of parts against each other.

INERTIA

The way the bowl spins or moves along the water also shows another principle of physics, that of inertia. Every object set in motion tends to continue its motion. Thus the bowl set spinning tends to continue to spin at the same speed. The bowl pushed along the water tends to continue moving along the water in a straight line at that same speed.

Of course, there is some friction between the bowl and the water, even though it is very little. Eventually a spinning bowl gradually slows down and stops rotating. In a similar way the straight line motion of the bowl when it is pushed across the water is also slowed by friction until the bowl comes to a stop.

Suppose the motion is fast. In that case friction is substantial. For example, a boat moving along the water at high speed must push the water out of the way very rapidly, and this requires much more force than at low speed. Violent waves are formed by the rapid motion, evidence of high friction in water. If the motor is stopped, the boat slows down quickly because of the high friction force. Then when violent waves are no longer formed, friction is greatly reduced and the boat gently coasts along the smooth water at low speed for a long distance.

The relatively low friction of a boat in water has had some interesting effects on the development of civilization. Low friction in water means that less force is needed to keep a boat and its cargo moving at steady speed. In addition, smooth rivers, lakes, and oceans provide free roadways on which boats can glide in any direction. As a result, the cost of transporting goods over long distances by boat is less than across land by any other known method. Thus many early civilizations tended to spread out along waterways, settling along rivers, lakes, and ocean coasts.

The first settlements in America were on islands and coastal regions. Not until hundreds of years later, after railroads had begun to develop, did large inland cities begin to grow.

Little did you realize when you pushed the bowl across the water of the bathtub that you were illustrating a scientific principle that left its mark on history.

STABILITY OF FLOATING OBJECTS

Place a wooden stick about 1 foot long in the water in a vertical position. Try to get it to float in that position. No matter what you do the stick will not stay vertical. It immediately tips over and floats horizontally. It is unstable in a vertical position and stable in a horizontal position.

Try the same thing with a capped empty vial. The vial is also unstable and will not stay vertical. It tips over and floats horizontally.

Add washers or coins to the vial, one at a time, capping it each time. Each added weight makes the vial float lower and lower.

After enough washers have been added there is no longer any problem about getting the vial to float vertically. It does so all the time by itself. Even if you tip over the capped vial so that it is horizontal, it always comes back to a vertical position. Now it is stable in a vertical position and unstable when horizontal.

In a similar way add weights to one end of the wooden stick without sinking the stick. Do this by tying heavy objects such as lead fishing sinkers or large nails to one end. When enough weight is added, the stick acts the same as the vial. It floats vertically.

Why does this happen?

First, note that wood is a material that floats in water. In other words, if immersed in water it has sufficient buoyancy to rise to the surface. Buoyancy is a force that acts upward. In the case of wood, the upward force of buoyancy is greater than its weight, and so it rises.

Now imagine the piece of wood, without weights on it, held in water at an angle midway between a horizontal and vertical position, as shown. What should happen to it when you let go?

We can obtain an answer if we consider what happens to the forces acting on the different portions of the stick (see page 108). One section (A) is completely out of the water. The water has no buoyant effect on portion A at

all. The only force acting on this part is the force of
gravity (arrow B), which tends to pull portion A downward without opposition of any kind.

An unstable position

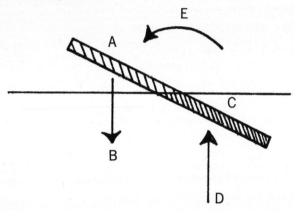

The rest of the wood (C) is completely under water.
As a result, there is an upward buoyant force on section
C greater than the downward weight of that part of the
wood. This difference, an upward force, is shown by arrow D.

Now observe the action of forces B and D on the piece
of wood. Force B, acting on the left side, tends to make
that side move down. Force D, acting upward on the
right, tends to make that side move up. The two forces
combine to make the wood rotate in the direction shown
by arrow E. This motion moves the stick toward a horizontal position. It is stable only in that position.

Let's analyze what happens when an object made of
dense material (F), but not heavy enough to make the en-
tire stick sink, is added to one end. The extra weight

makes that end fall through the water, as shown by arrow G, and the wood sinks much deeper than normally. As a result, much less of it is above water and most of it is under water. Since the main effect of the water on the wood is to provide buoyancy, the wood tends to be pushed up, as shown by arrow H. Now the two forces act to rotate the stick, as shown by arrow I, and it moves toward a vertical position. The extra weight at one end makes the stick stable only in that vertical position.

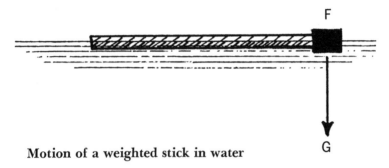

Motion of a weighted stick in water

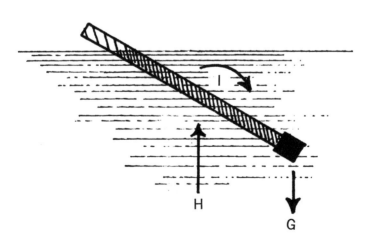

Suppose that we try to make the weighted stick rest in a vertical position with the weight on top, as shown. It is extremely difficult to set the stick perfectly vertical, and any small wave would tend to make it move slightly away from vertical. In that case, the heavy weight at the top tends to make that end move downward on one side, as shown by arrow J. At the same time the buoyancy (K) of the water acting on the lower part of the stick makes that end go up on the other side. The combination of forces turns the stick in the direction shown by arrow L. Once the stick reaches a horizontal position, the weight still makes that end go down. The stick keeps turning until the weight ends up at the bottom and the stick is in a vertical position.

An unstable position

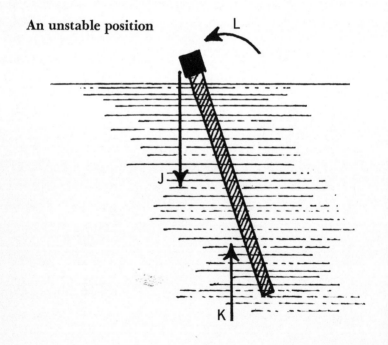

Designers must take such turning forces into account when planning new ships. Top-heavy ships have actually turned over during storms. In one case the captain had permitted lumber to be piled high on the decks, and this made the boat top-heavy and close to the point of instability. During a storm, the lumber shifted on the deck, causing the ship to tilt at a sharp angle. The ship then filled with water and sank.

Similar considerations apply to the ability of people and animals to remain vertical or horizontal. Human beings are top-heavy, with their weight much higher than the means of support, their feet. If a person leans over too far, his weight tends to topple him, just as the top-heavy stick in the bathtub toppled over. Nature has provided man with large feet, which furnishes some insurance against such toppling. But it requires a great deal of time in the infancy of human beings before one learns the difficult trick of balancing the body over one's feet and thereby remaining erect.

Four-legged animals have a much easier time of it. The horizontal position of an animal's body is more stable than man's vertical position.

You may think that the instability of man's support on two feet is a big disadvantage. It can be. On the other hand, man's upright position freed his two front limbs for handling things, and eventually led to tool-making and civilization. Some scientists think that this ability to walk upright played an important role in man's survival in the tall grass fields that covered many parts of the earth millions of years ago. He could stand up and look over the top of the grass to see the prey he stalked or his animal enemies. Then he could duck and move in the direction he wanted to go without being seen. You can see how the kind of forces that operate in the bathtub apply to man and his history and to other living things.

Brain Teasers
Answers appear on page 122.

1. What is the best place to store heavy objects in a boat? Explain your answer.

2. The catamaran is a wide boat that floats on two pontoons, one on each side. Why is this type of float advantageous?

Investigations on Your Own

1. Push a hollow floating ball under water in the bathtub and let go. Does it jump out of the water? Try the same thing with a piece of wood. Does it rise slowly or fast?

Find out why some floating objects rise much more rapidly when pushed under water and let go.

2. Investigate the shape of the surface of water in a rotating plastic or metal tumbler or bowl. One way to rotate the tumbler or bowl is to center it accurately on a phonograph turntable and then to turn on the phonograph.

Be sure to use an old phonograph and cover it with plastic in case any water spills. Also, use as little water as possible to avoid spilling and damage. Finally, begin with the slowest rotational speed on the turntable and see what happens before you go to higher speeds.

Answers to Brain Teasers

2

1. The distance between crests is 30 feet. This means that the waves are 30 feet apart. The waves pass by once every 4 seconds. Therefore, a wave must travel 30 feet in 4 seconds to reach the present position of the preceding wave. The speed is therefore the distance of 30 feet divided by the time of 4 seconds, 30/4, or 7.5 feet per second.

The end of the bay is ¼ of a mile away. One quarter of a mile is 5,280/4 or 1,320 feet. At 7.5 feet per second, the wave will reach the end of the bay in 1,320/7.5, or 176 seconds, or 2 minutes and 56 seconds.

2. Imagine the first wave coming out of the broadcasting antenna. At the moment it reaches a distance of about 1,000 feet from the antenna the second wave comes out. Both waves advance 1,000 feet and the third wave then comes out of the antenna. At the end of 1 second, 1 million waves come out of the antenna and they are

spaced 1,000 feet apart. Thus, the distance between the first wave and the one coming out at the end of 1 second is $1,000,000 \times 1,000$ or 1 billion (1,000,000,000) feet. Since this happened in 1 second, the velocity of the first wave is 1 billion feet per second.

How closely does this calculation fit the measured speed of radio and light waves—186,000 miles per second?

3

Answers to Brain Teasers, page 27

1. The clothing and flesh of people are soft and absorb sound waves more than they reflect them. Also the vertical positions of people sitting in seats produces a very irregular "surface," which tends to scatter sounds in all directions, rather than to reflect them in a regular way. By contrast, the seats and the floor are often hard and tend to reflect sound waves in a more regular manner. Consequently, when people are seated in an auditorium, there is reduced reflection of sound waves and greater irregularity in the reflections. This is why there is a difference in the way the music is heard.

2. Sound travels at a speed of 1,100 feet per second. (See page 23.) In 25 seconds sound travels $25 \times 1,100$, or 27,500 feet. This is about 5 miles. People generally do not connect the thunder that they hear with the flash they saw 25 seconds ago.

There have been explosions of volcanoes that were so loud that they were heard hundreds of miles away. In such cases the sound may not be heard for 15 to 30 minutes or so.

3. The speed of sound is about 1,100 feet per second. In 1.3 seconds the sound wave travels $1.3 \times 1,100$, or 1,430 feet. However, the sound must travel to the cliff and back. Therefore the distance to the cliff is half of 1,430 feet, or 715 feet.

4

Answers to Brain Teasers, page 42

1. The window does two things at the same time: it transmits most of the light (lets it go through) and also reflects some. First, consider the case when you are indoors. At night it is much brighter indoors. Therefore the reflection is much more visible than the very small amount of light coming in from outside.

During the daytime, however, there is much more light outside than inside. Therefore there is much more light coming into the house from outside than is reflected from the glass. As a result, the reflection is almost invisible, while objects outside are clearly seen.

With this information you can probably complete the explanation of what you observe outdoors, day or night.

2. There is no way to distinguish a perfect mirror image from an actual object just by looking at it. If you walk into a strange room that has a clean mirror along a complete wall, with no frame to outline it and make it appear to be a mirror, you have no way to distinguish the

images from real objects, just by sight. The images behind the mirror appear to be real objects, and so the illusion is created that the room is twice as large as it really is.

3. You see things clearly with the mask in place because there is a chamber of air in front of the eyes. Light is therefore refracted in its normal way as it passes from air into the transparent material of the eye. An image can therefore be focused by the lens of the eye on the retina, or light-sensitive area on the back of the eyeball.

But when the mask is removed, water touches the eyeball directly. The amount of bending when light passes from water into the lens of the eye is less than when it passes from air into the eye. As a result, the rays cannot be brought to focus on the retina by the lens, and the image appears blurred.

5

Answers to Brain Teasers, page 55

1. In northern Canada, near the magnetic pole, the north-seeking end of a magnet that is allowed to rotate freely up and down, as well as horizontally, points straight down. As the pivoted magnet is moved south, the angle gradually changes. In the northern United States it dips about 70°. In the southern United States, about 50°. Near the equator there is little or no dip. Consequently, a bathtub in Quito, on the equator, will be magnetized horizontally. The north pole will be at the

side of the tub that faces north, and the south pole will be at the side of the tub that faces south.

2. In Tierra del Fuego, at latitude 55°S, the south-seeking end of the compass tends to point south and downward toward some place under the Antarctic. So, the bottom of the bathtub will be magnetized south and the top north.

6

Answers to Brain Teasers, page 62

1. The volume of the pool is 60 feet × 25 feet × 4 feet or 6,000 cubic feet. We know that 1 cubic foot equals 7.5 gallons, so 6,000 cubic feet are equal to 6,000 × 7.5 or 45,000 gallons.

Water flows in at the rate of 1 gallon per second. Therefore, it takes 45,000 seconds to fill the pool. There are 60 × 60 or 3,600 seconds in an hour. Thus it takes 45,000/3,600 or 12.5 hours to fill the pool.

2. After 5 minutes, at a rate of flow of 4 gallons a minute, there are 5 × 4 or 20 gallons in the tub. This leaves 40 gallons to be added to reach the 60-gallon capacity of the tub. At the new rate of flow of 2 gallons a minute it takes 40/2 or 20 minutes to add the 40 gallons. The total time is therefore 5 + 20 or 25 minutes.

If the flow had not been reduced, the water entering the tub at a rate of 4 gallons a minute would have filled it in 60/4 or 15 minutes.

The extra time is 25 − 15 or 10 minutes.

7

Answers to Brain Teasers, page 70

1. If a life preserver is under water, its upward buoyancy is much greater than its weight because of its very low specific gravity, which is much lower than that of water. As a result, it exerts an upward force on anything attached to it (or holding onto it). Therefore, a person holding it is buoyed up out of the water. The person stops rising when the total weight of life preserver and person is equal to the weight of water displaced by the portions of both under water.

2. An object will always sink in a liquid that has a lower specific gravity and float in a liquid with higher specific gravity.

Kerosene (specific gravity 0.82) is less dense than water (specific gravity 1.00), and so will float on the water. Wax has a specific gravity of .90, which is less than that of water and more than that of kerosene. Since it is lighter than water and denser than kerosene, it floats on the water just under the kerosene.

Of course, you can't test a substance in this manner if it dissolves in kerosene or water. Try the experiment with kerosene, water, and wax. Does the wax remain undissolved?

What happens if you use a lump of sugar?

3. Archimedes solved the problem by putting an elephant on a flat raft and marking the depth to which the

raft sank. Then the elephant was taken off and replaced by bars of gold until the raft sank to the same level as before. At that position, the weight of raft plus gold was the same as that of raft plus elephant. Consequently, the gold had the same weight as the elephant.

8

Answers to Brain Teasers, page 80

1. Consider two equally warm cubic objects. Heat can escape from all six sides of each. But suppose that the block-shaped objects are pushed together to make one larger object. Two of the sides that formerly allowed heat to escape to the air are now joined, and heat no longer escapes that way. The rate of heat loss is reduced and the two combined objects cool off more slowly.

In effect, large masses have less surface area in proportion to mass (or weight) than do small ones. Since heat is lost through the outer surface, the chance for heat to be lost is less for the large mass. More of the heat is deep inside the object and less exposed to the air. Therefore, a large mass of hot material does not cool off as rapidly as a small one of similar shape.

2. Heating the liquid speeds up evaporation because the speed of the molecules is increased and they jump out more readily. A breeze on the liquid speeds up evaporation because it removes the molecules jumping out that otherwise have a chance to return. Pouring the liquid

into a vessel with a larger surface exposed to air increases evaporation because there is a greater opportunity for molecules to escape.

3. Evaporation of water is decreased on a humid day because there are already a great many water molecules in the humid air. As molecules of water jump out, some of them already in the air return to the water. The net effect of the returning molecules is to reduce the rate of evaporation. As a result, in humid air, there is less cooling effect from evaporation of sweat. The body then feels warmer because there is less loss of heat by evaporation.

9

Answers to Brain Teasers, page 88

1. The surface tension of the bubble pulls the bubble toward the wide opening of the pipe and then pushes air out of the mouth end of the pipe. The bubble shrinks.

2. The paper clip displaces a small amount of water, which then rises above the top level of the test tube. However, the water does not spill out because of surface tension, and the surface merely bulges a bit.

You can add many clips and create quite a bulge before the water spills over.

Why not try it? If you don't have a test tube, use any narrow vial or jar. If you get tired of adding clips you can drop coins into the water for faster results.

10

Answers to Brain Teasers, page 100

1. When you press down on the flexible top of a Cartesian Diver, you increase the air pressure inside. This increased air pressure forces more water up through the open bottom of the floating dropper, so buoyancy is less and the dropper sinks.

When the pressure is released, the squeezed air inside the dropper pushes the excess water out, the air in the dropper displaces more water, buoyancy increases, and the dropper rises.

2. Steam, boiling out of the water, pushes the air out of the can. Eventually the air pressure inside the can is replaced almost completely by steam under pressure.

When the can is sealed and removed, the steam is trapped in the can. The steam slowly cools and condenses to the much smaller form of water. This leaves no air or steam in the can. Consequently no air or steam pressure remains to counteract the outside air pressure of 15 pounds per square inch.

An ordinary 1-gallon can would have about 200 square inches of surface. Fifteen pounds per square inch on each of these 200 square inches produce a total force of 3,000 pounds, or 1½ tons—enough to crush the can.

The can is crushed slowly because it takes time for the steam to condense.

11

Answers to Brain Teasers, page 112

1. The weight should be stored at the bottom of the boat. Like the stick with the weight on the bottom, it is stable only if the weight is low. Of course, boats are built that way in the first place. The heavy engines are placed at a low position in the boat. The superstructure is made light and is never loaded with objects that are too heavy.

2. The wide base makes the catamaran very stable and almost impossible to turn over. As soon as one portion is pushed under water for any reason, buoyancy immediately pushes it up again.